It's Time to Turn Up!

It's Time to Turn Up! No More Trauma

LIFE CHANGE SERIES
VOLUME 1

Lady D

Flyte Time
PUBLICATIONS
INGLEWOOD, CALIFORNIA

Paperback ISBN: 979-8-9871789-0-4
eBook ISBN: 979-8-9871789-1-1
Library of Congress Control Number: 2022922111
Cover design and interior formatting by Open Heart Designs

According to Steven Pressfield, "Creative work is not a selfish act or bid for attention on the part of the actor. It's a gift to the world and every being in it."

Many people have graced the circumference of my life to see the unfolding of a childhood dream resuscitated by faith and belief for the greater good. This book is a labor of love and testimony about the power of faith and belief, to transform anything from good to great, on any given day.

The impetus to finish this project rests in part on an Instagram post by Michele Norris, one of the most trusted voices in the field of journalism. Michele's post read, "Keep going. The thing you are working on that some folks don't understand or can't comprehend is the thing that will expand horizons and create light and space for so many others who will be enriched by and grateful for your efforts. Keep going. The world needs you to keep going."

So, I continued to do what I set out to do: discover the truth and write about it.

To my son, daughter, and grandson, I hope this book finds a place in your heart.

A special thanks to Mae L. Clark, M. Nannette Marchand, and Irina Svistelina for your invaluable words of encouragement and support.

Contents

Some Assembly Required 65

A Special Note from the Author

—PSALM 23 (NKJV) *"The Lord is my shepherd; I shall not want. He makes me to lie down in green pastures.*

He leads me beside the still waters. He restores my soul. He leads me in the paths of righteousness For His name's sake. Yea, though I walk through the valley of the shadow of death, I will fear no evil. For You are with me. Your rod and Your staff, they comfort me. You prepare a table before me in the presence of my enemies. You anoint my head with oil. My cup runs over. Surely goodness and mercy shall follow me All the days of my life. And I will dwell in the house of the Lord Forever."

Many alumni of the foster care system have written about and inspired readers worldwide with stories of overcoming insurmountable odds. As an alumnus of the foster care system, I am the first to admit I lived the better part of my life encased in survivor's guilt, shame, and silence. These are the unintended consequences that cropped up as I made my way through the maze of a well-intended, yet trauma-inducing system.

For years I lived under a self-imposed code of silence powered by shame, an intensely painful feeling of believing I was flawed and unworthy of love, belonging, and connection. This belief was birthed by a series of traumatic life events experienced as a toddler, adolescent, and teen. But I never abandoned the search for words to give substance and meaning to my experience.

By creating space for faith to have her perfect work and become my writing partner, I decided to use my voice, a voice informed by seventeen years of lived experience in foster care, to write about the challenges, unspoken hurts, and routine slights encountered by children and youth as they make their way as non-consensual travelers through the highways and byways of foster care.

The ability to lend my voice to a conversation such as this arises from kinship rooted in a unique shared life experience, the unexpected and sometimes abrupt removal from our families of origin. The uniqueness of our experience appears in a statement by the Children's Law Center:

> "Nearly one hundred times a day, a child in California is placed in foster care. Los Angeles County alone has over 33,000 foster youth in care who have experienced abuse, neglect or been abandoned."

> "On any given day, there are nearly 437,000 children in foster care in the United States, and over 60,000 children in foster care in California."

The threads binding children and youth in foster care together are the *lack of voice* and *lack of choice* when it comes to expressing what they need to feel safe and secure and make the transition from surviving to thriving.

Over the years, I discovered our future, individually and collectively, is brighter than imagined. In the twenty-ninth chapter of the Book of Jeremiah, the creator of Heaven and Earth said, "I know the plans I have for you, plans to prosper you and not to harm you, plans to give you hope and a future."

In the absence of a relationship with kinship and family, a God-given hope and future are not a bad place to begin. *It's Time to Turn Up* and get on with living life with *No More Trauma*. We must reclaim our voices and pursue our God-given hope and future.

By harvesting the truth beneath our day-to-day experiences, we can position ourselves to wield our unique brand of magic and master the art of making peace with the past.

I will end my special message with a belief cultivated and used throughout the years to bounce back from every defeat, disappointment, delusion, deception, or distortion birthed by trauma:

"Irrespective of my current situation, or how my life began, I am not a lost cause or forgotten; I am a work-in-progress, a gift to the world."

You and I were created for such a time as this.

Introduction

It's Time to Turn Up, No More Trauma looks at pivotal events and turning points that shaped my life as a survivor of sexual violence and trauma, while demystifying the process for experiencing sustainable life change. This is the kind of change that provides protection in every season of life and accumulates spiritual wealth to distribute and share.

By writing, I am responding to a call to action to lead by example, while humbly acknowledging, like Kelly Noonan Gores, the author of Heal: Discover Your Unlimited Potential and Awaken the Powerful Healer, "It's no small task to demystify how we heal, not to mention articulate it in a way accessible to the masses." I hope the revelation of my truth will embolden survivors, and those who share a personal or business relationship with them, to do everything within their power to roll back the corrosive tide of dysfunction produced by traumatic life events.

The decision to memorialize my truth arises from the belief that there is power in owning our stories. This power enables the storyteller to make peace with the past and harvest truth to nourish and uplift future generations.

If someone asked, "What problem or problems does this book solve?" I'd say, "It invites women and girls emotionally disfigured by traumatic life events to take the lead in positioning themselves to experience better outcomes by changing the quality of their lives from the inside out." This book challenges readers to take a second look at their life, open the floodgates of healing, and make a conscious decision to incorporate the following practices into daily living.

- Embrace adversity as a teacher, not an enemy or foe
- Reframe hurtful events as opportunities for growth
- Embrace and make use of their God-given gifts and talents
- Narrate and update their life story to align with truth
- Affirm their worth as a gift to the world

The ability to incorporate these practices into daily living might appear like a tall order after years of butting heads with a hard-knock life, but nothing is beyond reach when pursued with faith and belief. Frederick Phillips said it best, "It is often hard to distinguish between the hard knocks in life and those of opportunity." But I believe readers can move mountains by heeding the advice offered by world tennis champion Arthur Ashe, who said, "Start where you are, use what you have, and do what you can."

This is not a bible study or deep dive into scripture, but a chronicle of life events written to reveal how four key scriptures framed and changed my life from the inside out. Those scriptures are Jeremiah 29:11, Psalm 23, Psalm 71, and Proverbs 3:5-6. Other passages appear throughout the book to demonstrate my reliance on scripture to mend stress fractures in my heart, mind, body, soul, and spirit to create an inner sanctuary called home.

As a teaching memoir, this book unfolds in three parts: Part I—Life Shifts and Transitions, Part II—Creating Order Out of Chaos, and Part III—Some Assembly Required. Each section offers a candid look at memorable and pivotal events of my foster-care experience between ages five and eighteen. The decision to look back arises from a desire to extract insight and wisdom worthy of paying forward and to obliterate the perpetuation of generational dysfunction and family misfortune.

This book also offers insight and wisdom conveyed through my life story. But a shift in focus, tone, and voice occurs in the middle of Part III to transition from shining a light on me to intentionally shifting the spotlight to you, as I transition from past to present and bring this book to a close.

Rather than summarize what to expect from each section, I've included blank pages to use any way you'd like as an integration tool to get the most out of this book to make your interaction and engagement with the material, personal, purposeful, and practical. As a reader, you bring something unique and distinct to the page. Your thoughts, opinions, and impressions matter.

If you are a trauma survivor or have crossed paths with someone who self-identifies as one, you might see yourself or someone you know in the pages of this book. If at any point while reading you feel the need to pause for reflection or take a breather for your health, please do so. But first, use a pen, pencil, or favorite marker to:

- Jot down an insight you'd like to explore further
- Highlight an idea or topic you'd like to share with a family member, friend, or co-worker
- Commit to doing something in the name of self-care to avoid a mistake or pitfall observed in the text

These are simply suggestions. Feel free to add anything that will yield a positive return on your investment of time and set the stage for experiencing positive life change. I hope you will use the space provided to identify and amplify issues and concerns that resonate with you.

One parting note before moving on: In the interest of unveiling truth without offense, the people associated with the underlying events are not named.

— PART I —

Life Shifts and Transitions

PSALM 31:1 (NKJV)
The Lord a Fortress in Adversity
In You, O Lord, I put my trust;
Let me never be ashamed.

CHAPTER 1

Truth Be Told

"I have come to believe over and over again that what is most important to me must be spoken, made verbal, and shared, even at the risk of having it bruised or misunderstood."

—AUDRE LORDE, POET AND AUTHOR

*M*s. *LORDE'S PERSPECTIVE CONVEYS THE* motivation behind the decision to take my place among the throngs of women and girls, both in and out of foster care, who are survivors of sexual violence. The kindred spirits I'm lining up with know how it feels to lug shame and pain around like a carry-on bag, as if we are frequent flyers going somewhere. But our elevation and ascension to greatness will never occur if we remain grounded by memories no one wants to talk about, much less acknowledge.

But Tarana Burke, a diamond in the rough, cut through the silence to give sexual abuse survivors like me a voice when no one wanted to listen to our stories, let alone give us the mic. In 2006, Ms. Burke, an advocate for women in New York who experienced rape at seven years old, coined the hash tag and the movement *#MeToo* to empower women who had endured sexual violence by letting them know they were not alone—that other women had suffered the same experience.

The response was especially meaningful for people who work with survivors of sexual assault and harassment. The grassroots effort Tarana Burke spearheaded expanded to reach a community of survivors from all walks of life. The silence surrounding sexual harassment and assault no longer exists, thanks to Ms. Burke. The notes for Chapter 1 include contact information for the MeToo Movement, which offers a free online series created for survivors, by survivors, to help them navigate crisis and trauma and begin to rebuild a sense of safety, joy, and purpose.

The past I never spoke about or revealed to anyone, not even those closest to me, including my children, caught me off guard the day I discovered an exploratory study about girls ages four to seventeen living in foster care. The study revealed:

- 81 percent were sexually abused
- 68 percent were abused by more than one person
- 98 percent were subjected to multiple assaults
- 50 percent of the assaults lasted two years or more
- 36 percent involved non-penetrating genital contact, and
- The average age for the onset of abuse was five years old.

The study identified a pattern of behavior I immediately recognized:

- A violation of body space
- Sexually aggressive remarks
- Sexual touching without permission
- Genital contact
- Fondling

The more research I conducted, the more I realized I did not stand alone. There were hundreds, if not thousands, of girls like me who were pursuing healing and freedom from a sexually abusive past. This past restricts freedom of expression in every way, especially voice, choice, and how we show up.

Herman Law, the nation's leading law firm for victims of sexual abuse, specializes in fighting for the rights of victims in foster care. The firm offered insight into the breadth of the problem by sharing a summary of investigations conducted by states, institutions, and universities on the occurrence of sexual abuse in foster care:

> Johns Hopkins University conducted a study of a select group of foster care children in Maryland. This study showed that foster care children are four times more likely to experience childhood sexual abuse than their peers not in the foster care setting. The study also found that children in group homes are twenty-eight times more likely to be sexually abused.
>
> Oregon and Washington State studies found that nearly one-third of foster children reported that a foster parent or another adult in the home abused them.
>
> In New Jersey, researchers completed various investigations into foster care abuse, concluding that "no assurances can be given" that foster children are safe in the state. The New Jersey Office of Child Advocacy completed a report that found 36.5 percent of sexual abusers were foster parents.
>
> A study of multiple cases in metropolitan Atlanta found that 34 percent of foster children experienced abuse, neglect, or other harmful conditions.
>
> In 2013, a series of FBI raids across the United States that recovered child sex-trafficking victims found that more than half of the children were from foster care or group homes.

My eyes bulged when I discovered a news story about a woman previously cared for by the child welfare agency that failed me and two other chilling accounts of sexual abuse.

- July 2021—A woman sued the Los Angeles County Department of Children and Family Services, alleging she was sexually abused as a child by her foster father and two foster brothers. Impregnated by a brother at thirteen, she alleged her caseworker arranged for an abortion, and returned her to the home where the abuse continued for two years.

- May 2021—A nine year-old girl was allegedly molested and raped by her foster father for years, impregnating her at the age of fourteen. The DNA evidence proved the father raped and impregnated the girl. After giving birth, she remained with the family as the abuse continued until departing at seventeen.
- June 2016—A foster father admitted to regularly supplying his daughter with cannabis and conceiving two children with her at ages sixteen and eighteen.

After reading these stories I experienced another kind of Me Too moment, #WTF. This is the reality I uncovered when I set out to make sense of my experience.

I received practical advice as I traveled back in time to hook up with my younger self while reading a book by Haemin Sunim, *The Things You Can See Only When You Slow Down*. In looking back, I set out to uncover the blind spots that caused me to veer away from myself and neglect self-care practices to protect and serve my true and authentic self. In the words of Angeles Arrien, "Wisdom is the reward for honest self-confrontation, and it is the quality that often emanates when you begin to uncover your true face."

Notes

CHAPTER 2

Breaking and Entering

"When you abuse someone, you limit their perspective, and you trap them in your view of them or your view of the world."

—TARA WESTOVER

ACCORDING TO THE U. S. DEPARTMENT of Health and Human Services, Substance Abuse and Mental Health Services Administration (SAMHSA), "Trauma results from an event, series of events, or set of circumstances experienced by a person that has lasting adverse effects on their mental, physical, social, emotional, or spiritual well-being." This definition established a framework for honest dialogue and candid conversations about the relationship between trauma-inducing events and behavioral health, among stakeholder groups that included trauma survivors, practitioners from an array of fields with experience in trauma treatment, researchers focused on trauma-specific interventions, policymakers in the field of behavioral health, and federal, state, and local service providers funded through trauma focused grants and initiatives.

According to SAMHSA and the national experts who helped craft this definition, trauma knows no boundaries. It affects the lives of people without regard to age, gender, socioeconomic status, race, ethnicity, geography, or sexual orientation. Trauma represents a widespread, harmful, and costly public health problem, occurring because of acts of violence, abuse, neglect, the death of a loved one, the loss of a friend, natural disasters, gun violence, mass shootings, wars, and emotionally harmful experiences.

After identifying the personal and social origins of trauma, the panel acknowledged, "The public institutions and systems created to provide services and supports to individuals are often themselves trauma inducing," citing the abrupt removal of a child from an abusing family as one such example.

The abrupt removal from my mother's care when I was eleven months old represents the initial trauma-inducing event that adversely affected my sense of safety, security, and well-being. My brother, a year and two months older, shared in the experience. The narrative pieced together about the reason for our removal indicates the child welfare agency received an anonymous tip about two toddlers at home alone.

True or not, the removal triggered a rapid series of placements in foster care. I do not have a way to validate what transpired in the early days following displacement. But I distinctly recall the foster home we moved to at the age of five. My family consisted of a husband, wife, and son older than my brother and me.

The care from my first caregiver, Lady P, created an opening for experiencing unconditional love. My memory arises from the tone and timbre of her reassuring voice. She welcomed the dawn of each day with a veiled greeting, "Good Morning Sunshine!" To this day, I still appreciate the impact of her comforting spirit. I get goose bumps when I reflect on the slightly worn hands that gently combed, brushed, and braided my hair. Her small frame, wispy hair like mine, and marble-shaped eyes created a mother-hen vibe. I followed her like a baby chick, reaching for her hand and hopping on her lap at every chance.

A photo of me in pigtails wearing a light pink dress with matching bows made by Lady P for a kindergarten class photo graces my home. My stay with Lady P lasted a little more than a year. The memory of our time together remains among my prized possessions.

But I have less-than-fond memories of her son who handled me like a possession—a plaything or doll to rub, touch, and forcefully bump into without guilt or remorse. During playtime in the backyard or while hanging out in the garage, Lady P's son violated my space by touching and rubbing my genital area. I felt filthy and gritty, like the dirt beneath my feet. More than anything I felt like a traitor for concealing the truth from Lady P, pretending all was well when it was not. If nothing else, I knew Lady P's son was a jackass.

I think his jackassery represented a twisted way of exacting payment for sharing his mother with my brother and me. On the other hand, his aggressive and disrespectful behavior may have reflected a way to collect payment for hitching a ride every now and then in his go-cart. Whatever the case, I became an object of sexual violence through behavior that laid the foundation for behavioral health issues. According to the authors of *The Long-Term Effects of Childhood Sexual Abuse: Counseling Implications*, "Sexual abuse occurs whenever one person, an adult, or older child dominates and exploits another by means of sexual activity or suggestion."

The exposure to sexual violence added a second layer of trauma to the garden variety of child abuse allegedly committed by my teen mother. My entanglement with the child welfare system added a third layer to the labyrinth of traumatic life events experienced before the age of ten. This trifecta of events shattered and stole my sense of security, safety, dignity, and self-worth.

Just when I thought things could not get worse, at the age of six, I transitioned to another foster home within walking distance of Lady P. My new home, run by a Christian couple with a biological son and daughter, included a trio of foster siblings—two brothers and a sister. The sheer number of people the matriarch cared for reduced my chances of replicating the unconditional love I experienced with Lady P. I started to wonder, *Will I ever feel special and loved again?*

Lady B, my second caregiver, moved about with little or no pep in her step. She wore muumuus and house dresses purchased from K-Mart, White Front, and Zody's. In all my days, I never saw her break a sweat as she glided through the house as if riding a magic carpet. Now I know why—there was no need to fret. The County of Los Angeles paid her a pretty penny to extinguish the panic attacks and flashbacks of children committed to her care.

Her expertise shined brightly as an executive chef. She never left us begging for bread. If I could go back in time, I'd award her a medal of honor for the vigilance displayed in protecting the refrigerator and food pantry. Like a bald eagle, she kept an eye on the fake cheese, powdered milk, eggs, no-name peanut butter, and canned goods received from the government. She excelled in keeping our hands off the ingredients to execute meal plans.

When not chain-smoking, bossing us around, or barking orders about chores, Lady B exhibited signs of parental attention deficit disorder. Her waking hours revolved around the telephone, daytime TV soap operas, and eating. But I learned a thing or two from observing her obsessions. If there was ever a time to sleep with one eye open, this was it. I developed a habit of keeping an eye on the potential predators in my midst, my non-biological brothers, ages eleven and fifteen.

I'm grateful the fellas kept their distance during the first couple of months. But as time progressed, the situation changed. Common occurrences like sitting next to one another at the dinner table, church, in the car, or on the sofa while watching television created an opening for the commission of acts of sexual violence. Who would think engaging in slip and slide on the front lawn, playing pool, table tennis, or flag football, or passing someone in a hallway would trigger an urge to reach out and touch someone?

I initially passed them off as nothing more than incidental contact. But my feelings changed with the frequency and intensity of bumping up against me for no reason, pressing a thigh into mine leaving no wiggle room, genital touching, and fondling of body parts reserved for a mother's touch while dressing or bathing a daughter.

Even when confined space was not an issue, the bruise brothers, as I began to call them, crashed the outdoor patio gatherings I staged with imaginary friends just for the hell of it. They never bypassed an opportunity, when beyond the line of sight of Lady B or my brother, to make sexually suggestive comments. The older of the two, under the guise of needing help cleaning his room, never failed to gain permission for me to help. Unaware of the risk posed by the setup, Lady B obliged, leaving me alone in his presence. But for the tears pooling in my eyes, I believe an act of sexual violence beyond bumping, touching, and fondling of my genital area would have occurred.

The violation of my space and acts of sexual violence continued until the bruise brothers began to focus on girls their own age. But I never understood how a brother, biological or foster, could turn a relationship into an opportunity to get their kicks at another's expense. The objectification of my body changed me from the inside out, which I will discuss later. While we are on the topic of brothers, it hurts to admit that my own brother offered little or no protection. He faded into the background of the unfolding trauma. The faraway look in his eyes signaled that we lived in different worlds. I think the separation from our birth mother wrecked him from the inside out.

I could continue to walk down memory lane recounting the acts of sexual violence endured while living in foster care, but I won't. Suffice it to say, my experience set the stage for showing up emotionally disfigured with blind spots that affected my perspective and ability to make choices and decisions to protect and serve my mental, physical, social, emotional, and spiritual well being.

Notes

CHAPTER 3

The Greatest Heist of All Time

"Forgive yourself for everything you didn't know in the past. Don't waste any of your precious energy beating up yourself or anyone else. Your power to change your life is in the present, regardless of your past."

—CHRISTIANE NORTHRUP, M.D.

THE OPENING QUOTE SHINES A light on the path survivors of sexual violence must take to see a better day. Forgiveness is not optional. But I bristled at the thought of forgiving myself or anyone else for what happened. As a ten year old, I did not possess the strength to extend forgiveness or revive a heart hardened by sexual violence. How could I forgive myself or anyone else for something I did not understand? Every day, without pressing play, these questions popped up, *What did I do to bring about the situation I'm in? and Why did these bad things happen to me?*

Each day I stretched, bent, and contorted my mind into every shape possible to make sense of what happened to the five-, six-, seven-, eight-, nine-, and ten-year-old versions of me. God knows I entered the world with the same gifts as everyone else: curiosity, creativity, and imagination. But with the passage of time, all three disappeared as I morphed into an accidental poster child for sexual violence.

To cope with the unsettling change in stature, I adopted a repertoire of habits, tactics, strategies, and defense mechanisms that owe their existence to the old dirty bastards (ODBs) birthed by trauma: *Deception, Defeat, Delusion, Disappointment, and Distortion.* The defining characteristics of this bunch include a lack of agency[1] and voice, as well as a restricted range of motion for freedom of expression. Lack of agency manifested with my willingness to roll with the punches, even if the punches knocked me out. My adoption of a victim-of-circumstances mentality restricted my ability to speak up, and when I did, it was with a beaten-down and battered voice that failed to attract listeners.

For better, or for worse, this is how the ODBs influenced how I showed up for family, friends, peers, and myself after enduring six years of sexual violence.

Habits

The fear of Defeat led me to neglect the benefits of sleep and turn my back on the Good Shepherd watching over me. I experienced a lot of sleepless nights because my internal body clock remained on high alert to monitor the whereabouts of the bruise brothers. The lack of sleep undermined my ability to manage anger and rage. So at least once a month I fought and mixed it up with someone in the neighborhood or a classmate over a petty incident. It's easy to get riled up when you are worn out and tired.

The ODB named Disappointment baited me into living under a code of silence about what happened to me. This silence progressed into a low-grade, debilitating state of depression. Because I felt unworthy of accomplishing anything great, I aborted hobbies, pastimes,

---

1 Agency—The new hip word, meaning one realizes and uses their power to further their ends. https://www.urbandictionary.com/define.php?term=Agency

and creative endeavors that made me happy, including playing the violin. My relationship with myself turned out to be the biggest stumbling block encountered over the years.

Tactics

The ODB named Deception taught me how to pull off disappearing acts, to remain low key, incognito, and below the radar at family gatherings, social outings, and church functions. I picked up this tactic to keep people from getting close to me. I thought they might see the layer of taint, disgrace, and shame covering me, the source of the ODBs in my life.

Before I became a poster child for sexual violence I sang and danced my butt off! But I owe the ODB named Deception for the theft of joy. I stopped moving, grooving, singing, and dancing, afraid rhythmic movements of my body might attract unwanted attention.

Strategies

The Delusion arising from the belief that I bore responsibility for keeping the peace at all costs led me to put the needs of others ahead of myself. In retrospect all I can say is, "WTF is up with that?" This strategy changed me from the inside out by leading me away from self-care practices to maintain my dignity and self-worth.

I have the ODB named Distortion to thank for persuading me to repeatedly run away from home after beatings, to hang out and hideout in the restroom at the neighborhood park, the stacks in the library, a pitch-black alley, or the restroom of a mom-and-pop restaurant. There were days when the thought of checking out and yielding to the end of life brought more appeal than living. The means of checking out didn't matter, but I envisioned options like intentional drowning, abduction by a stalker or streetwalker, or facing off with a fast-moving truck or vehicle. Some days I slipped away unannounced after completing my chores, walking the streets for hours, searching for a whiff of freedom, while sipping on a bottle of Schweppes Bitter Lemon.

Defense Mechanisms

Researchers say survivors of sexual violence often develop coping mechanisms to protect themselves from the memory of their experience. These mechanisms can manifest in confusion, denying the effects and impact of an experience, or difficulty expressing feelings. After years of abuse, I showed little to no emotion for myself or anyone else, including my non-protective brother. I pulled the kill switch and shut off my emotions.

The greatest heist of all time occurred when the ODBs ganged up, hovered overhead, and dropped a bomb on me for every level of trauma experienced by letting me know, "You do not matter," "You are not worthy of love," and "Your best days are over." In response, I developed a tick that caused me to withdraw, pull back, and cringe when someone attempted to display genuine love and affection.

It appeared the good-for-nothing ODBs gained the upper hand by sowing seeds of distrust in every area of my life, including me. My behavior and actions created an endless cycle of suffering, so I decided to ditch the wretched habits, tactics, strategies, and defense mechanisms birthed by trauma.

I decided to try a little tenderness and give forgiveness a try. Psychologists define forgiveness as "A conscious, deliberate decision to release feelings of resentment or vengeance toward a person or group who has harmed you, regardless of whether they deserve your forgiveness." But forgiveness does not gloss over or deny the seriousness of an offense. When you forgive, no matter your age or life stage, forgiveness does not forget, condone, or excuse what transpired. But forgiveness does empower you to recognize the pain you suffered without letting that pain define you, enabling you to heal and move on with life.

I wanted to know what forgiveness could do for me. What benefits could she offer to replace the habits, tactics, strategies, and defense mechanisms birthed by trauma? At a minimum, she could set the stage for a new beginning. She could teach me how to stop replaying past hurtful events like an old mix tape. She could help me break the habit of crafting scenarios from dated material that set me up for a lifetime of tripping and falling, like a victim of circumstance, into a pit of helplessness.

In the sixth chapter of Luke, verses 43-45 (NKJV), I am told a tree is known by the fruit it bears. As an eleven year old who intellectually entrusted her well being to the Good Shepherd but rejected Him by her behavior, I remained fruitless for some time. The season for bearing fruit, according to Galatians 5:22-23 (NIV), in the form of love, joy, peace, forbearance, kindness, goodness, faithfulness, gentleness, and self-control, had not arrived. Years passed before I opened my heart to forgiveness and allowed her to settle in to regain the upper hand to orchestrate the rhythm of my days and nights.

Notes

CHAPTER 4

Healing Is a Choice

> *"Making a commitment to healing involves two steps: the first is admitting that healing is necessary, and the second is opening yourself to the information that you begin to attract following the acknowledgement."*
>
> —CHRISTIANE NORTHRUP, M.D.

W*HILE FORGIVENESS INDEED OFFERED BETTER* options, I remained dazed, confused, and a tad bit angry as a pre-teen because Lady B and her husband remained clueless about the abuse occurring under their roof. Yet, neither could feign ignorance nor deny the radical change in my behavior. One day, the girl my foster parents knew, the one with the big brown dreamy eyes who excelled in everything she put her hand to—board games, sports, music, dancing, and playing violin—abruptly ditched her favorite pastimes. In exchange, their daughter assumed a guarded and armored presence fueled by anger. This presence dared anyone to come near—parents, teachers, church folk, biological and foster siblings, classmates, and would-be friends.

Up until this time, the negative effects of trauma trickled in like raindrops; a tad bit of dysfunction here, a tad bit there, but never dysfunction everywhere. But the defining wound produced by my exposure to trauma, an aversion to touch, physical contact, and vulnerability, suddenly appeared. The unfolding of everyday life revealed the indelible affects, which neither I nor anyone else could deny.

As a pre-teen, it did not take much to arouse the pain coursing through my veins. The defining wound devoured the trust to build meaningful connections. Whenever someone reached out to touch or hug me, I crossed my arms, creating a barrier to keep them at bay. The slightest touch—hostile or friendly, malignant or benign—rekindled memories and flashbacks to scenes of abuse the unsuspecting person knew nothing about.

At eleven, I experienced an unexpected burst of anger and turn for the worse. The defining wound destroyed the innate sense of joy that comes with waking up to welcome the dawn of a new day. Even though I lacked words to convey what I felt, I knew why victims of abuse blow a fuse and bust a move to put their abusers out of their misery. If I were asked to toss out a word to capture my feelings, I'd choose rage.

The intersection of anger and rage exposed a chink in my armor. The thought of sucking up and pardoning the bruise brothers for their behavior represented acts of diplomacy and forgiveness beyond my reach. The thought became too much to bear. I erased the bookmark in my Bible highlighting the fourth chapter of Ephesians, verse 26 (NKJV), which says, "Be angry, and do not sin: do not let the sun go down on your wrath." I set out to defend my honor, even the score, and give the bruise brothers their just deserts

When circumstances required our mutual presence, I snarled, growled, and gritted my teeth as I called the bruise brothers everything but their given names in a profane way under my breath. When either invited me to play a game of table tennis, pool, or caroms, I seized the opportunity to inflict bodily harm. I transformed the pool stick or tennis paddle into a weapon to smack a shoulder, arm, elbow, hand, anything within reach to get my licks in. I felt vindicated by the discomfort and looks of surprise, but the invitations ceased when the bruise brothers realized my behavior originated from revenge, not seizures.

After cutting me off, I moved to Plan B, which entailed vandalizing and ransacking their room at every opportunity just for the hell of it. I wanted the bruise brothers to know what an invasion of privacy felt like. I proceeded to cut up and destroy anything of sentimental value, baseball caps, collectible cards, comic books, favorite T-shirts, and socks. It was just my way of expressing my sentiments about their worth as pure and simple trash. Sometimes, I hit them where it hurt by carting off and redeeming for cash empty soda bottles hidden in their room. At other times, I played the role of spy and troublemaker. When either brother said or did something that smelled like trouble, I ratted them out to Lady B. Sometimes I played Devil's advocate. I made things up just to watch them squirm during the criminal investigation launched by Lady B.

The sense of vindication dissipated when I regained my senses and acknowledged two wrongs don't make a right. No matter how hard I tried, the balance of power never shifted between the bruise brothers and me.

But I experienced a change in standing with Lady B. My living out loud and acting out cost me big time. My behavior attracted her ire and landed me in therapy at a community health center. I did not resist because the radicalization arising from the theft of my dignity and self-worth turned me into someone I barely knew.

But forging a relationship with someone new was not something I looked forward to. Researchers and clinicians acknowledge children exposed to trauma and adverse childhood experiences may have difficulty forming healthy and stable relationships during their teen and later years. The exposure can also affect how they show up for themselves.

Participating in therapy placed me at the center of a game of truth or consequences. I could tell the truth about what happened or keep my mouth shut. I opted to show up like a game show contestant more interested in winning the war on words than truth telling. At the end of our first session, I started to question the wisdom of sharing my secret with a total stranger. For someone I just met and only knew for a hot minute, was it safe to share?

At the second and third sessions, I did my level best to abort the process and sever our connection. I told the therapist, "My mom's worried about me, but I'm okay. I can take care of myself." The therapist ignored me and continued asking a series of probing and exploratory questions from a list attached to a clipboard. No matter the question, I responded with words aimed to please rather than trigger alarm. I impressed myself with meaningless answers crafted to steer clear of the heartbreak, anger, and pain pulsing through my veins.

I continued to show up and share trumped-up stories rooted in imagination, not reality. In the process, I mastered the art of curating whitewashed BS. Like an escape artist, I glossed over merciless beatings, acts of sexual violence, and atrocities no child should endure while living with a biological or foster family. The soundtracks of life produced for therapy sounded good, but never revealed the truth about my experience.

Our bi-weekly sessions emitted the touch and feel of a funeral procession and chair-side burial service where I interred negative feelings, disturbing emotions, and unwanted parts of myself. Little did I know my antics created a living hell for the unwanted parts of myself to dwell only to rise and live again later in life.

I buried the truth because I did not trust my therapist enough to let her into my world. Even when I thought about crossing over to the land of truth-telling, fear of the unknown beckoned me to play it safe and suppress everything for the sake of marking time and staying alive.

The repeated breaking and entering of my privacy for six years deprived me of the ability to trust, so I chose to live with the consequences of non-disclosure. Speaking up carried risks that exposed me to one or more of the following consequences:

- Separation from my brother
- Relocation to another foster home with no guarantee of a better outcome
- Rejection of my truth because I lived with a Christian family
- Physical attack by Lady B's daughter
- Turning the tables to accuse me of lying to gain attention

My silence all but guaranteed an unhappy ending to my first crack at therapy. I walked out of the final session dazed, confused, and a tad bit angrier. Angry at myself, more than anyone else, because I veered away from a path of self-care to protect, serve, and heal myself and break free from a victim of circumstances mentality. I let the defining wound etched on my heart by trauma make me appear powerless and small.

Even though I blew the chance to out my abusers, I walked away with two helpful lessons. One, that healing is a choice no one can police or enforce and two, the internalization of anger never works out for your good because anger creates a blind spot that obstructs your ability to see.

Notes

CHAPTER 5

Look Who's Talking

"Our lives begin to end the day we become silent about the things that really matter."

—DR. MARTIN LUTHER KING, JR.

IF OUR LIVES TRULY BEGIN to end the day we become silent, then I had my work cut out for me. I lost the antithesis of silence— voice—a long time ago. The loss began at the age of five, continued to dissipate from ages six to ten, and totally disappeared by the time I entered therapy at eleven.

VisualThesaurus.com provides a visual display of words to convey how we use our voices in daily life. The following words convey the importance of voice as it pertains to this chapter.

- Call Out
- Cry Out
- Express
- Say
- Shout Out
- Utter
- Verbalize

On any given day, we use our voice to vocalize, articulate feelings, and communicate how we think or feel about something. Voice also includes the thoughts we think, the actions we take, the decisions we make, our manner of dress, how we move and use our bodies, how we treat one another, and how we choose to spend our time. But the pains of life entered in to complicate the use of my true and authentic voice. The voice I needed to articulate what I experienced as a victim of sexual violence.

Over the years, these are the things I learned: silence occurs as a matter of habit not conscious deliberation; silence is hazardous to your health; and silence will not hold you hostage any longer than you permit. I also learned from personal experience about the mental health risks associated with silence. The failure to speak up disfigured me emotionally, impairing my ability to do the following:

- Speak up and make myself known
- Communicate and make healthy choices
- Articulate my priorities and preferences
- Say yes to life
- Say no to abuse
- Own my story
- Make sense of my experience
- Resist enslavement to self-defeating behaviors
- Intercede and cry out for me and my inner child

All of this to say that silence is a pitiless killer, a killer who does not extend mercy to the holder of secrets. I can count the events and circumstances leading to the end of freedom of expression in my life on both hands, but not one rivals the corrosive and damaging consequences associated with silence, because our words have power.

According to Sienna Chu, LMHC, each of us has an inner child, a younger version of ourselves who holds our earliest experiences, thoughts, and beliefs about both ourselves and the world around us.

Ms. Chu makes a point of noting this inner child may have varying degrees of unmet needs, gaps in relational bonding, or a lack of trust in oneself and others. When we don't do the healing work to better understand and meet these needs, our inner child can unconsciously sabotage our lives and relationships.

In looking back, I realize the act of self-betrayal committed in therapy created an opening for my inner child to rule and reign. Two blind spots emerged when I abandoned the use of my true and authentic voice. The first created space for the unattended wounds of my inner child to fester and metastasize. The second placed an ill-equipped child in the driver's seat to navigate the terrain of a life adversely affected by trauma. The marks of disqualification included a limited range of emotional experiences, little to no imagination, and a propensity for knee-jerk reactions. I have no one to blame but myself for the consequences of my decision. But I have my inner child to thank for the choices that created a living hell for me.

My inner child, powered by low self-esteem, lacked the maturity to serve my best interests, so I vacillated between feelings of joy and shame, an intensely painful feeling of being flawed and unworthy of love, belonging, and connection. Shame made it difficult to look others in the eye. William Shakespeare said, "The Eyes are the window to your soul." Without knowing anything about William Shakespeare, shame led me to avoid eye contact whenever possible. I believed other people could see the part of me damaged and tainted by sexual violence. So, in elementary school, I followed the lead of my inner child around and often found myself at the end of cafeteria school lunch lines or fading into the background at school assemblies, recreational outings, and community events.

I spent the better part of elementary school hiding behind the fear of coming out as a foster child, because my inner child said, *Do you really want to talk about your dysfunctional foster family, or draw attention to the fact you don't know jack about your own?* A debilitating sense of stupidity descended when someone asked, Who's your mamma?, Where's your daddy?, and How many brothers and sisters do you have?

As a student, I devoured textbooks and consumed library books for extra credit like snacks. But when a teacher sought volunteers to answer questions, shame led me to slump down in my seat, lower my head, and clasp my hands to keep from showing up. This happened even though I knew my ability to analyze and solve complex problems exceeded that of my classmates.

But my eyes lit up with joy when asked to join a game of volleyball, softball, or basketball. The collaboration reflected the epitome of family, a collection of people bound by a willingness to show up for one another and compete with the best. Team sports created a sense of normalcy and connection because my teammates did not know I lived in a foster home or anything about the unspeakable events occurring where I lived.

But whenever I entertained the thought of making friends, shame led me to believe I did not have what it takes to make the transition from teammate to friend: trust, transparency, and vulnerability. So, when the school bell rang or the game clock signaled the end of play, I returned to my seat or made my way home to hang out with my inner child plagued by shame, trust issues, and low self-esteem.

Even though the unmet needs of my inner child led me to pull up short in making friends, one day I kicked her to the curb like a bad habit and decided to forge a connection with a classmate, who became my guardian angel. Our favorite pastime involved a weekly stroll to the drug store on Sunday to purchase candy before making our way to church, where I learned to care for my mind, body, soul, and spirit.

Our Sunday stroll turned into a weekly ritual for receiving insight, wisdom, and encouragement to manage the indignities of daily living. The touch, feel, and sound of a church congregation filled a gap created by the loss of kinship and family. No matter the topic, I always departed with an understanding better than the one I entered with, and an ever-increasing faith in a Good Shepherd watching over me.

When we arrived at church, we greeted the ushers and paid respects to church mothers before hightailing it to our favorite seats in the balcony to get a good look at the pastor and choir. One Sunday the pastor directed our attention to 1 Corinthians 13:11 (NLT), which says, "when I was a child, I spoke and thought and reasoned as a child. But when I grew up, I put away childish things." Each word felt like a needle pricking my skin, with each word pricking a little harder until I decided to straighten up in my seat. I bit down on a Lemonhead while trying to figure out what the passage had to do with me.

As I moved the candy around in my mouth, the essence of my childish ways made a debut: dumbing down in class, running from making friends, hiding out in plain sight at social events, building walls to keep people out, ransacking rooms, stealing soda bottles, lying about my brothers, and turning the therapist's office into performance theatre. After taking it all in, I decided to ditch the childish ways and pity parties thrown by my inner child.

I don't recall the exact words used to convey my decision, but I decided to stop aiding and abetting the presence of trauma in my life. I followed up by pulling the plug on the survival techniques and coping mechanisms curated by my inner child. I regained the driver's seat and severed our connection to thoughts, attitudes, and beliefs that functioned like a battery pack to fuel enslavement to learned dysfunctional behavior.

I didn't kill my inner child, but I cut the juice fueling her connection to a lesser version of what she could become with my help. In time, I regained full use of my true and authentic voice while coaching my inner child into becoming a cheerleader and champion for wholeness and healing. The life-changing tools of *self-awareness*, *acknowledgment*, and *reflection* created just enough space for me to flip the script, because the Bible says, "God" has not given us a spirit of fear, but of power and of love and of a sound mind."

——— *LIFELINES FOR FEARLESS LIVING* ———

At times life seems unfair because bad things happen to good people, like you and me. Abuse of any kind constitutes an invasion of privacy, and restricts our freedom of expression, but I'd like to share a few life-affirming lessons learned throughout my experience:

1. We can rise again and get on with living life when we face the truth about our circumstances.

2. We can experience freedom from guilt when we acknowledge we are not responsible for what happened to us.

3. We can move forward when we allow forgiveness to have her perfect work in our relationships, tests, and trials.

4. We can heal what we allow ourselves to acknowledge and feel.

5. We can show up as our true and authentic self by reclaiming our voice.

Notes

— PART II —

Creating Order Out of Chaos

PROVERBS 3:5-6 (CEV)

With all your heart you must trust the Lord and not your own judgment. Always let him lead you, and he will clear the road for you to follow.

CHAPTER 6

The River of Fear Runs Deep

"As painful as it may be, recognizing, but not dwelling on tragedy and the role it plays in our lives is a sign of maturity."

—ANNETTE GORDON-REED

IN THE QUEST TO LIVE beyond the revolutions of my past, I discovered it's empowering to reframe events through the lens of truth. When I reflect on days gone by, I see pivotal events that contributed to my growth or demise. The most important lesson learned along the way is adversity is a teacher, not an enemy or foe.

If memory serves me right, as a toddler I learned to walk without difficulty or challenge. But the long walk towards freedom from the adverse effects of trauma caught me by surprise. After regaining the driver's seat and reclaiming my voice, I experienced an unnerving shift in equilibrium. If you've ever lost balance when rising from sitting in the same spot for too long, you know the feeling. I had to learn how to walk because the river of fear runs deep, well below the realm of consciousness.

The questions bubbling up amid my newfound freedom included:

- Who and what will I be now that I'm free"
- How do I fight the impulse to return to familiar self-destructive behaviors?
- If adversity is a teacher, what lesson or lessons does she want to teach?

My questions prompted a flashback to how my ancestors must have felt on January 1, 1863, the day the Emancipation Proclamation set them free from slavery. Booker T. Washington, in *Up From Slavery*, recalls the scene as he gathered with family to hear the unexpected announcement.

When slaves were told we were all free and could go when and where we pleased, for some minutes there was great rejoicing, and thanksgiving, and wild scenes of ecstasy. The wild rejoicing on the part of the emancipated coloured people lasted but for a brief period, for I noticed that by the time they returned to their cabins there was a change in their feelings. The great responsibility of being free of having charge of themselves, of having to think and plan for themselves and their children, seemed to take possession of them. It was very much like suddenly turning a youth of ten or twelve years old out into the world to provide for himself. In a few hours, the great questions with which the Anglo-Saxon race had been grappling for centuries had been thrown upon these people to be solved. Was it any wonder that within a few hours the wild rejoicing ceased, and a feeling of deep gloom seemed to pervade the slave quarters?

This excerpt offers a glimpse into a world characterized by jubilation and fear. While some gathered family members and personal belongings to strike out on their own, others hightailed it back to the plantation. The idea of turning a youth of ten or twelve years old out into the world to provide for himself resonated with me. The day I reclaimed my voice I gained my freedom, but I did not know how to be me.

Decades later, Marianne Williamson, the author of *A Return to Love*, penned words that captured my conflicted feelings. According to Ms. Williamson,

> Our deepest fear is not that we are inadequate. Our deepest fear is that we are powerful beyond measure. It is our light, not our darkness that most frightens us. We ask ourselves, "Who am I to be brilliant, gorgeous, talented, fabulous?" Actually, who are you not to be? You are a child of God. Your playing small does not serve the world. There is nothing enlightened about shrinking so that other people will not feel insecure around you. We are all meant to shine, as children do. We were born to make manifest the glory of God that is within us. And as we let our own light shine, we unconsciously give other people permission to do the same. As we are liberated from our own fear, our presence automatically liberates others.

I knew I had everything to gain and nothing to lose by liberating myself from an enslaving past, but I had junk in the trunk to sift through and process.

In between waging war with my foster family, I struggled with separation anxiety and survivor's guilt arising from the loss of my biological mother and brother. The separation from my birth mother triggered the onset of separation anxiety, which covered me like a mist that never lifted. The deprivation stoked a fear of abandonment and rejection by peers, creating an obstacle to making friends.

They say survivor's guilt occurs when you survive a life-threatening situation and someone else dies. In my eyes, my brother died the day he turned his back on me by departing to live with another foster family. My ten-year-old take on survivor's guilt might appear weird, but the severance of our connection created a palpable and real sense of guilt and isolation.

At other times I experienced nightmares, threatening the enjoyment of my newfound freedom. The two nightmares I distinctly recall involve a knife-wielding infant reaching to sever her mother's umbilical cord, and a girl emerging from a bush with a mummified corpse in pursuit. I did not attempt to interpret either dream, but each reflected the status of my connection to my biological family: severed and dead.

Even on my best day, the effects of separation anxiety and survivor's guilt made it difficult to show up as anything but a hot mess. But one day I decided to try something new. I started toying with the gifts of the spirit - curiosity, creativity, and imagination.

Even though I cannot explain what happened to change me from the inside out, I experienced a surge of energy, igniting a desire to create new ways of showing up for myself, my foster family, classmates, and peers. Creating new ways of showing up offered a way out of the debilitating rut of going through the motions doing the same thing and expecting a different result. Like a good teacher, adversity coaxed me out of my comfort zone to tinker with the possibility of living a better life by doing what I stubbornly refused to do in the past:

- Speak up for myself
- Make myself known
- Make-life-affirming choices
- Verbalize my priorities and preferences
- Say yes to life
- Say no to self-defeating behaviors

As a girl who wanted to experience breakthrough more than anything else, I rolled out like this to get a taste of freedom.

- I responded to my brothers' cheesy smiles and sinister grins by telling them, "Get lost and go stuff yourself!"
- I built a support network at church by serving as a greeter, candle lighter, and junior usher.
- I continued to play softball, handball, and volleyball and ran track to hone my skills as an athlete and competitor.
- I engaged in arts and crafts during summer months.
- I took up bike riding to distance myself from a house full of memories I'd rather forget.
- I negotiated a cease-fire with Lady B to end the purchase of clothing from Zody's and K-Mart that made me look like a court jester at school and church.
- I threw a pair of white and black, pointed-toe, patent leather spectators on top of the school roof, which no one retrieved, to convey my distaste for the look.
- On Saturdays after completing my chores, I visited a reading room managed by a church to study the Bible and learn more about the Good Shepherd watching over me.

My actions might come across as child's play, but what I accomplished laid the foundation for becoming the head and not the tail, a leader not a follower. Adversity taught me how to lay down the defensive weapons of war acquired to shield myself from future hurt and pain, so I could pick up and wield life-affirming offensive strategies and tactics.

By allowing adversity to teach me a thing or two, I discovered a way to rebuild my dignity and self-worth, important keys to becoming me, even when others did not approve or agree. Step by step and bit by bit I learned how to walk and talk like the free girls around me.

I resisted the temptation to return to my former ways by mimicking the behavior observed among prayer warriors and healers at church. Whenever I felt the urge to hightail it back to my comfort zone or when I sensed a brother about to invade my space, I lifted an index finger and with all my might said, "Loose here devil!" From observing prayer warriors and healers, I learned that these words, when spoken with power, authority, faith, and belief, restore freedom and release from tormenting thoughts and malicious attacks. I spoke these words as needed to expand an ever-increasing freedom from haunting memories produced by separation anxiety, survivor's guilt, and a not-so-distant, enslaving past.

Notes

CHAPTER 7:

What's in a Name?

"As our struggles mature, they produce new ideas, new issues, and new terrain on which we engage in the quest for freedom."

—ANGELA Y. DAVIS

WHENEVER SOMEONE ASKS, "WHAT'S IN a name?" I say, "Everything," because a name adds flavor, character, and uniqueness to our existence. But the child welfare agency robbed me of all three when attempting to establish my identity after separating me from my birth mother. Rather than obtain a birth certificate bearing my given name, *Donita*, which means *World Mighty* and *Lady*, someone decided to recreate my name by adding a vowel and reordering the letters of a phonetically perfect name, resulting in *Donetia*. By doing so, the child welfare agency exceeded its authority, because my given name established my identity, irrespective of the decision to separate me from my birth mother.

The misspelling created a linguistic challenge, an enigma others had to solve. When I entered foster care, I did so with a name that put others to test, offering seven distinct ways to pronounce my name. The ensuing pronunciations sounded like anything but music to my ears. Most of the time I felt the speaker did their best to make sense of the letters strung together by the child welfare agency.

The inexcusable trauma-inducing error made me stand out even more as a foster child. I racked up unexcused absences by failing to respond during roll call because I did not recognize the sound coming out of the speaker's mouth. Sometimes my name bounced around like a beach ball, until a classmate pointed a finger to alert a teacher to my presence. The frown that emerged upon hearing my name prompted others to tiptoe around my identity crisis. The misspelling created a sore spot and source of irritation I have yet to contend with in a satisfactory manner.

But I learned to co-exist with the humiliation of a butchered name by taming the urge to clap back when offended, insulted, or slighted by pronunciations that did not meet my auditory expectations. After latching on to the life skill of *emotional literacy*, I stopped tripping over the indignities of the misspelling and weird pronunciations.

If someone asked me to describe emotional literacy in my own words, this is what I would say: "Emotional literacy casts a lifeline to reel you in when you find yourself about to drown in emotionally deep and treacherous waters." The starting point for successfully trafficking in this life skill requires fielding curveballs thrown by family, friends, and peers with a mind free of fretfulness and panic, or a desire to control or forcefully manipulate outcomes.

According to Claude Steiner, a pioneer and subject matter expert in this area, emotional literacy is about understanding your feelings and those of others to facilitate relationships, using dialogue and self-control to avoid negative arguments. Emotionally literate people manage their emotions in a way that improves their relationships, enhances their personal power, and boosts their quality of life.

I used this life skill to lessen the impact of the sting of invisibility arising from the mispronunciation of my name. The misery associated with invisibility as the world swirls around you makes you feel like the walking dead. But I used the lifeline offered by emotional literacy to revive and build rather than tear down relationships by responding with empathy and compassion rather than anger and rage.

I gained valuable information by learning to read the room at home, school, and social gatherings by observing facial expressions, body language, hand gestures, and tone to discern a speaker's motive and intent. Were they making fun of me, or were they doing their best to grapple with the enigma posed by my name?

I even created space for levity and humor by embracing a nickname given by a classmate that made me smile, *Donut*. The name originated from the recognition of my ability to roll with teammates through thick and thin when suiting up as a competitor. I found humor in the antics of class clowns who got a kick out of throwing my name around to vex and annoy when I learned not to expect much from those with high ratings on the uncouth end of the emotional literacy spectrum.

I learned to sit with the discomfort of showing up with a jacked-up name by managing my emotions, watching my mouth, and meditating on ways to live up to my given name, Lady. This strategy made me feel old, but I decided to order my steps around the peace and calm of showing up in an emotionally literate manner.

The growth spurts experienced by reigning in my emotions prompted the creation of an acrostic to support my desire to create space for living with *HEART*.

Hope inspired me to believe all things would work out for my good, no matter what.

Endurance empowered me to keep putting one foot in front of the other.

Ambition motivated me to use my gifts, talents, and skills.

Resilience fueled my ability to bounce back from setbacks and disappointments.

Truth challenged me to see myself as a gift to the world.

The change in thinking and acrostic offered a way to remain steadfast and unbothered by things I could not change—a misspelled name and class clowns.

While writing this book, an encounter occurred to remind me, decades later, that the struggle to say my name is real and persists. During a chat with a beloved colleague at the end of a shift, my colleague apologized for embracing me for months without uttering my name for fear of getting it wrong. Her confession arose after hearing our manager address me in the way I preferred, irrespective of spelling. I received my colleague's confession with understanding and empathy. When I invited her to share her best impression, the response produced a smile because it lined up with the failed attempts of so many others. My smile also signaled peace with bearing a name that produced the sound of something delicious and tasty, like a dish you might want to try while dining out.

In looking back, I distinctly recall the day I hooked up with the essence of my given name. It happened on the last day of work before launching into a two week vacation to celebrate Christmas. A co-worker passed by to drop off a handwritten message that read:

"Merry Christmas Lady D.
See you when I return. You are one of God's Angels.

Love Ya
Alicia

I regained the essence of who I am through a heartfelt message scribbled on a slip of paper from an Allstate Insurance Company notepad, bearing the company slogan, "You're In Good Hands."

That day marked the rebirth and resurgence of the real me, *Lady D.* I'm not superstitious and I do not believe in random acts of kindness or coincidence. But the message received continues to pay dividends. It restored the honor, dignity and identity misappropriated by the child welfare agency.

Notes

CHAPTER 8

Let's Get Ready to Tumble

"You're meant to create and grow and change. In order to do that, you sometimes have to go through discomfort."

—CHRISTIANE NORTHRUP, M.D.

AS A FOSTER KID, I set my sights on improving my life by any means necessary. I graduated from high school with honors at sixteen and believed education would open doors of opportunity for me like the ancestors, elders, and kindred spirits I read about in *Ebony* and *Jet* magazines.

After graduation, I continued to work part-time at Jack in the Box and spent my free time immersed in the soul-stirring lyrics of my all-time favorite album, *Home*, by Stephanie Mills. At sunset, I hooked up with my Boo to party into the wee hours of the night. Naïveté led me to believe my worst days were over, but nothing prepared me for the bombshell that destroyed this line of thinking.

One afternoon while lying in bed reading, Lady E, the matriarch of my fourth foster home, knocked on the door. I lowered the book, turned down the music, and told her to come in. After entering, she shoved the album covers lying at the foot of the bed into a pile before taking a seat. She started tapping the tips of her fingers together and breathing deeply. I thought, *Maybe she's sick. She could be pregnant, or angry about me coming in late.*

After ten to fifteen seconds, Lady E opened her mouth and pursed her lips, but nothing came out. Without taking another breath, the finger tapping stopped and Lady E said, "Baby Girl, you can't live with us anymore because you're not in school." She folded her fingers as if to pray and proceeded to say, "I don't know what to do, I didn't make up the rules."

I sat up straight and said, "Whoever made the rules must be a fool." A simple warning about the dangers of graduating early would have allowed me to course correct and extend my stay by intentionally failing classes, skipping school to generate a truancy violation, or doing something crazy to earn a long-term suspension.

I tried to minimize the impact of the agency's decision by putting on a strong face. I knew Lady E would never do anything to harm me, but her bedside chat shook me up. No matter how hard I tried, I could not stop tears from pooling in my eyes. Lady E departed quietly to give me privacy. I leaned back and tried to recall the instructions on what to do in the event of an earthquake. But I knew a drop, cover, and roll maneuver would not protect me from the aftershocks generated by our chat.

The impending relocation to a group home for girls brought back memories of what it felt like to be shipped back and forth over the years like cargo. The pain accompanying each transition felt like undergoing an amputation without anesthesia. But in times of distress like this, I leaned on the forty-first chapter of Isaiah, verse 10 (NIV), to remember how to respond as a child of God. "Do not fear, for I am with you; do not be dismayed, for I am your God. I will strengthen you and help you; I will uphold you with my righteous right hand."

Even though this passage lightened my load, I did not look forward to undergoing another round of separation, severance, and loss. Somewhere I read that upheavals, a sudden change or disruption, have a purpose. They usher in new beginnings, but I did not want new. I wanted to remain rooted and grounded in the place I had called home for the past three years.

The thought of parting ways with roommates who happened to be friends led me to remain low-key for the remainder of my stay. I felt ashamed and embarrassed about taking a step forward to finish high school, only to experience a bureaucratic response that set me back three steps, maybe more. I numbed out in advance by skipping family dinners, feigning illness to avoid interacting with people, and requesting more work hours to decrease time with friends and family.

The decision to send me to a group home for girls pissed me off, because a group home provides a restrictive placement option for children and teens in foster care with emotional or behavioral problems. I struggled to comprehend the placement decision, which I equated to cruel and unusual punishment.

Within a matter of weeks, a caseworker showed up to pick me up. After exchanging dry pleasantries, she inventoried my belongings and started placing them in her car. I paced back and forth to make sure she didn't trash anything. After the last trip, I opened the door of the bucket out front, strapped myself in, and raised a hand to say goodbye to Lady E. The sight of her leaning against the house like she needed someone to prop her up lingered for some time.

The road trip to the group home, an undisclosed location, occurred without music or small talk, amid the sound of an air conditioner, with bated breath and passing cars. The lack of small talk and silence reflected the position and stature of children and teens in foster care. We do not have a voice or a choice about who we live with or for how long.

During the ride, I threw a side-eye or two to convey my displeasure with the relocation effort. A tinge of bitterness crept in while reflecting on the havoc wreaked by the child welfare agency in the life of children and teens like me.

I pressed my feet into the floorboard to ground myself and refrain from giving the caseworker a piece of my mind. I redirected my attention to the word received the day Lady E dropped a bomb on me,

Isaiah 41:10. The recollection kept me from telling the caseworker what she and the child welfare agency could do with themselves.

We approached a street sign that read, Welcome to West Adams Heights. Our road trip ended in front of a weather-beaten, brown, two-story house. The caseworker rang the doorbell and a house parent with huge eyes and a fascinating goiter opened the door and motioned for us to step inside and bear left. The furnishings in the living room looked like something purchased from the *Antiques Roadshow*. Everything showed signs of heavy use and abuse. I caught a whiff of something shouting for a blast of Lysol or Febreze. After scanning the room for a place to sit without vanishing, I chose to sit on an ottoman.

During the intake and orientation process, I completed a walk-through and got a peek at my room, while learning my roommates consisted of a pair of sixteen and seventeen year olds. We returned to the living room where I signed the house rules. I shoved the papers in the direction of the caseworker and said, "Adios, Hasta Luego," before heading upstairs to unpack before the others returned from school.

Notes

CHAPTER 9

Spinning Mixed Messages

*"Our most difficult relationships offer us the greatest opportunity
for growth and change."*

—SUSAN L. TAYLOR

*R*ELOCATION TO THE GROUP HOME for girls offered me
everything but a fresh start. I met my roommates as they trickled in
from school, representing African-American, Indigenous, Hispan-
ic, and Asian-Pacific families. I'll never forget the raucous laughter
that erupted when I introduced myself and shared how I ended up
in the group home for girls. The unsettling reception conveyed con-
tempt for the milestone I achieved by graduating from high school.
The raised eyebrows and shaking heads communicated rejection and
disrespect for the audacity to show up without an arrest record or
criminal history to parse and compare. The chilly reception made
me realize it is not easy fitting in when you stand out.

But what I lacked in the way of criminality, I made up for
in exposure to traumatic life events, the cement binding our
lives together. The events responsible for our fortuitous introduction included everything from family violence, criminal
behavior, incorrigibility, juvenile delinquency, substance abuse,

child abandonment, child neglect, sexual abuse, and parental misconduct. Our separation from family created common ground for bonding and conversing in a superficial way about boys, the latest fashions, romance, and music, but not much else.

The tone set on day one dashed any hope of connecting with my roommates based on vulnerability, transparency, and trust. If anything, the hostile reception I received strengthened my resolve to keep to myself and peacefully co-exist in a place lacking the touch and feel of home. But my line of thinking presented a challenge because nothing in my life up to this point, good or bad, shut the door on wanting peers in my life to support, uplift, and encourage me.

According to the founders of the Asheville Academy for Girls, a leading therapeutic boarding school dedicated to helping girls overcome emotional and academic challenges, "For many teenage girls, peer relationships take priority over everything else." Living in a group home managed by a house parent like a fast-food restaurant elevated the importance of connecting with someone other than myself. In addition, the fear of missing out weakened my resolve to stay in my lane. The available options for navigating my stay included:

- Making myself a priority and loving my roommates to the best of my ability
- Following in the footsteps of my roommates, and
- Bracing for the sting of rejection if I kept to myself

My options reflected the difference between choosing yourself and adopting the ways of peers. Merriam-Webster Dictionary defines peer pressure as doing the same thing as other people of the same age or social group to gain their respect and acceptance.

According to Brené Brown, author of *The Gifts of Imperfection*, "Authenticity represents the opposite of peer pressure. It consists of a collection of choices we make every day, to show up, to be real, to be honest, and to let our true selves be seen. Staying real is one of the most courageous battles we'll ever fight. Choosing authenticity is not an easy choice."

Instead of choosing myself, I allowed fear-based decision-making to rule and reign. I caved in and decided to follow my roommates to gain a sense of connection, acceptance, and approval.

After making my decision, I quickly lost count of the number of times we snuck out of the house after curfew by descending the stairs at the rear of the house to hook up with boys. I narrowly escaped developing a criminal record when a trip to the drug store to buy snacks turned into an hour-long detention and interrogation. I had no reason to believe the trip posed a risk. But while I cruised the magazine aisle to thumb through the latest edition of *Teen Star*, surveillance cameras caught my roommates stashing items in their backpacks. Our detention triggered a call to the group home. When the house parent arrived to negotiate a release, the store manager agreed while informing her to expect a criminal filing alleging petty theft against everyone but me.

Whenever we were not violating curfew, we hopped on a bus to make an appearance at recreational outings, concerts, house parties, and pot-smoking dens. Between our travels, we hung out with adults who provided food, shelter, and beverages to engage in underage drinking. The hours disappeared while we smoked cigarettes, puffed on marijuana, and sipped on a communal bottle of Boone's Farm Strawberry Hill, Silver Satin, or Thunderbird. When the good stuff ran out, we transitioned to six-packs of Colt 45, Old English 800, and Schlitz malt liquor.

My introduction to alcohol and drugs provided an escape from shame, which manifested in upper-body tension to remind me of my status as a victim of sexual violence. I self-medicated to ease the discomfort, but the dawn of a new day proved sobering by exposing the futility of trying to outrun the past like footprints in the sand.

For six months, I justified going along for the ride by telling myself, *Girl, you deserve to have fun and do your thing after all the crap you've been through.* But with time, I questioned my commitment to living a better life because my words became nothing more than sound bites for paying lip service to a dream.

The activities and outings associated with our connection did not line up with how I viewed myself. I knew from an early age my life mission and purpose revolved around uplifting, encouraging, and motivating others to reach their full potential. I sensed the inclination to lead was a gift, because nothing about my wretched life qualified me to serve in this manner. But within six months, I transitioned from a leader to a follower and from the head to a tail.

The influx of guilt arising from mixed messages communicated by my behavior turned out to be more painful than the prospect of rejection. One day something greater than guilt punched me in the gut to initiate an about face and return to my true and authentic self. The revelation led me to see that peer pressure, if left unchecked, leads to self-destructive behavior, poor decision-making, lapses in judgment, and choices that do not serve your best interests. I seized the change as an opportunity to negotiate a new connection with my roommates based on authenticity and healthy boundaries.

The fragile and self-serving connection I forged six months earlier took a turn for the worse. My decision to withdraw from participation in late-night and weekend activities set everything in motion. The backlash from reneging produced eye rolling, whispered conversations, and isolation. One evening after stepping out of the shower, I heard the ringleader say, "She thinks she's smarter and better than us," while another chimed in, "Dat bitch thinks she's too cute to hang out with us!"

I did not clap back, even though their cruelty and comments hurt, because I had created the situation I sought to undo. I used the occasion to create a walking meditation and reminder; no matter how intense a disagreement or conversation gets, "Do no harm, just LOVE unconditionally, Leave Others Viable and Edified."

The demolition and rebuilding of our connection remained a work in progress for weeks. My attempts to reestablish a connection based on authenticity unfolded in fits and starts. But my efforts ceased when I grasped the futility of attempting to move the needle beyond frenemy status. I learned that the task of creating space for authenticity versus blending in to avoid isolation or rejection is not for the faint of heart.

Susan L. Taylor, in her book *Lessons in Living*, says "Our relationships are our mirrors; they reflect where we are in consciousness. And if we are willing to face the truth about ourselves, our relationships offer lessons that lead to our greatest transformation." I decided to let the transformation begin with me by extracting what I learned from my experiment with peer pressure.

- Putting the needs of others ahead of yourself comes with a cost, identity theft, and the loss of self-esteem, self-worth, and the power of choice.
- There's a significant difference between embracing others in the spirit of love and ignoring your best interest to gain acceptance and approval.
- It takes courage to admit when you make a mistake.
- It takes humility to course correct and get back on track.
- Positive life change begins with right thinking.
- Our thoughts dictate our actions and behavior.
- Our most difficult relationship is the one we have with ourselves.

Notes

CHAPTER 10

Ready, Set, Glow

"With courage, nothing can dim the light that shines from within."

—MAYA ANGELOU

MY *STAY AT THE GROUP* home for girls served as a breeding ground for a worldview I still cling to: *My life is a gift to be mined for the treasure that lies within.* I knew I possessed something special to light up a room, but I needed help removing the obstacles dimming my light. Help arrived in the form of a psychiatrist who stopped by monthly to conduct group and individual therapy sessions. Mental health professionals say participating in a group can offer insights into things we cannot see because we are too close to a situation to view things objectively. But the lack of ground rules to govern the flow of interactions during group left little room for the benefits to manifest.

So, I set my sights on faring better in individual therapy. After several sessions, the psychiatrist concluded separation anxiety contributed to my heightened irritability, fluctuating sense of self-worth, and recurring mood swings. Even with the discovery of my Achilles heel, I turned down the offer for meds to stabilize my moods.

I received advice on how to navigate without losing myself to peer pressure again or going to the other extreme and becoming antisocial. But I didn't receive anything on how to heal a broken heart caused by the loss of kinship and family, or how to uproot the shame birthed by sexual violence. After several months, I felt like a walker on a treadmill, racking up miles but going nowhere. At the end of each session, I departed the way I entered, unsure about a cure for my condition.

The lack of resolution led me to think long and hard about ways to calm my emotions when I tripped over questions like, *How do I put one foot in front of the other, when there's no mother, father, brother, or sister in sight?* or *Who do I turn to in times of need?* I recited the Serenity Prayer provided by the psychiatrist to roll back waves of tormenting thoughts when I did not receive an answer, "God, grant me the serenity to accept the things I cannot change; Courage to change the things I can; and wisdom to know the difference." But I needed something more than a prayer to keep me from ending my life.

While my roommates attended school, I read a Bible found in a nightstand in my room. The group home did not offer free writing pads or pens like hotels, so I converted the blank pages separating the sixty-six books of the Bible into a journal. I used the pages and a pen seized from my part-time job to write love letters and prayers to God. Even though I did not attend church while living in the group home, I knew from experience by attending church while living with Lady B that the Bible offered clues for making sense of my life.

One day I camped out in Chapter 139 of the Book of Psalms (NIV), written by King David, a man who experienced victories and failures, triumphs and tragedies far greater than mine. King David, in speaking with God after acknowledging Him as an all knowing, seeing, and present creator of all things, affirmed his own worth by declaring, "you created my inmost being; you knit me together in my mother's womb. I will praise you because I am fearfully and wonderfully made." King David's boldness prompted me to take a second look at my life.

I discovered affirmations have the power to shape the outcomes we experience if we believe in the power of the words to bring about an expected end. According to the developers of the *I Am* app for smartphones,2 "An affirmation is a simple but powerful statement that helps strengthen the connection between your unconscious and conscious mind." Affirmations remind me of solar-powered lights installed to automatically light up when darkness descends. Affirmations emit light to remind us of who we are when we are challenged by rejection, tormenting thoughts, or despair because we are unable to resolve a personal, relationship, or family matter.

Armed with the belief God did not break the mold when He created King David, I started to believe I entered the world fearfully and wonderfully made, not a mistake, accident, or afterthought. I found a reason to live and not give up in the power of King David's declaration. By reframing my experience, I started to believe nothing could separate me from the love of God and dim the light shining within. I grabbed a pen and started stringing words together to replace tormenting thoughts with affirmations based on what the Bible said about me:

- I am fearfully and wonderfully made
- I am more than my past
- I am beautiful, powerful, and creative
- I am a gift to the world
- I am a work in progress

With each repetition, I dug a little deeper to reclaim fragments of my life that I thought had been laid to rest. With repeated use, I accomplished much more than imagined.

---

2 https://monkeytaps.net/

- I removed the dark clouds produced by survivor's guilt and separation anxiety dimming my light.
- I exchanged the loss of kinship and family for a never-ending relationship with the creator of Heaven and Earth.
- I cast my cares about the shame birthed by sexual violence onto the shoulders of the Good Shepherd watching over me.

I gained access to the treasure that lies within by creating affirmations to meet my every need. I kept the light within shining bright by harvesting the spiritual meaning of my experiences. With time, I discovered that God uses imperfect people to model and minister wholeness and healing to others. He does so by empowering imperfect people to become reservoirs of compassion, faith, and belief. And asking them to live, love, and lead by example to help others succeed by incorporating the following practices into daily living:

- Embrace adversity as a teacher, not an enemy or foe.
- Reframe hurtful events as opportunities for growth.
- Elevate authenticity to its rightful place as the starting place for cultivating meaningful relationships.

If harvesting the deeper meaning of current or past events is something that resonates with you, here are a couple of suggestions.

- Create affirmations to shine a light on the truth of who you are
- Journal about your hopes, dreams, and aspirations
- Read the Book of Proverbs, a practical book dealing with the art of living
- Download the *I Am* app for smartphones
- Search for yourself in the pages of the Bible

——— LIFELINES FOR FEARLESS LIVING ———

I believe adversity, like rain, falls into every life, as a drizzle, shower, or torrential downpour. But we possess the power to pivot, shift, and change the quality of our lives from the inside out by wrapping our minds around a couple of building blocks. These building blocks take the form of beliefs that can transform tragedy into triumph by affirming the following things:

1. We can create order out of chaos by walking *through* the valley of the shadow of death casts by the lesser version of ourselves.

2. We can build better relationships with ourselves and others by using the life skill of emotional literacy.

3. We can rejoice in the dawn of a new day by embracing change and transition as a way of life.

4. We can live our best life by showing up as our authentic self, not someone else.

5. We can navigate the storms of life by anchoring our hopes and dreams to faith and belief.

Notes

— PART III —

Some Assembly Required

JEREMIAH 29:11 (CEV)
*I will bless you with a future filled with hope
—a future of success, not of suffering.*

CHAPTER 11

We Become What We Behold

"Wake up every day knowing your value and believing in your worth."

—SKYLAR DIGGINS-SMITH

Journal Entry

Two years have passed, I'm seventeen years old and still living in the group home for girls while holding down a part-time job. At night, I scroll through the Bible to pass time and eavesdrop on the recap of my roommates' weekend activities. The anticipation and excitement of turning eighteen and attending college turned me into a word nerd. I expand my vocabulary by devouring throwaway newspapers, Penny Savers, and junk mailers retrieved from the garbage. I don't have a library card to take a deep dive into the imaginary world of a fictional writer, so I recycle reading material while dumpster diving.

A COUPLE OF MONTHS BEFORE MY eighteenth birthday the house parent asked me to step into her office. My sense of humor kicked in. As I made my way to the office, I pictured her asking if she could depend on me to keep a secret and not rat her out for sleeping on the job after the others departed for school. The grin on my face turned to a frown when I sensed something serious about to go down.

While wringing her hands and massaging her knuckles, the house parent said, "When you turn eighteen the agency will terminate your placement and declare you an emancipated teen." Which I interpreted as a bureaucratic way of saying the agency would stop taking care of me. The irony of the decision sucked. Seventeen years earlier, the agency relied on an anonymous tip to justify removing me from my birth mother's care. But years later, the agency announced its plans to abandon me without looking at how the withdrawal of support would affect me.

In a matter of months, I would become a ship without a rudder, a house without a home, and a star without a planet. My rite of passage as an emancipated teen would unfold without support—no food, no shelter, or money to keep me from becoming homeless or turning into a beggar, panhandler, sex slave, or whore to make ends meet.

The responsibility for deciding what to do with the rest of your life after weaving and bobbing to the rhythms of the child welfare system for seventeen years proved to be a mind-bending experience. To steady my gait for the long walk toward self-sufficiency, I owned my story. But with livid vehemence, I refused to accept and buy into the looming tragedy set in motion by the decision to terminate my stay.

I contained the fire burning within by biting my tongue to keep from fussing, cussing, and plotting schemes I might not live to regret. I extinguished the rage coursing through my veins by pausing to think about Proverbs 13:3, (AMP) which says, "The one who guards his mouth thinking before he speaks protects his life; The one who opens his lips wide and chatters without thinking comes to ruin." In other words, tough times call for tough measures. As a girl with a short fuse, some called *Hot Pockets*, I had a reputation for blowing up when things did not turn out as planned. So, I created some commandments to keep from imploding and making a bad situation worse:

- Do not let anger ignite a fire that consumes the unseen blessings and grace of God.
- Do not let grief arising from the situation turn inward and become the sword I die upon.
- Do not let disappointment short-circuit the emotional bandwidth required to assess my predicament with common sense.
- Do not allow bitterness to take root and create a stumbling block, causing me to pull up short in achieving my dream of living a better life.

I managed to keep my anger from boiling over and tainting my dwindling stay by latching on to a word of encouragement shared by Steven Covey, an American educator, author, and entrepreneur, who consistently encouraged his followers to face adversity and hardship head on by declaring, "I am not a product of my circumstances, I am a product of my decisions."

In the weeks leading up to my departure, I grounded myself in uplifting affirmations to maintain sanity and exercise agency over my life. The affirmations sounded something like this:

- I rise strong everyday
- I keep my eyes on the road ahead
- I walk by faith believing the Good Shepherd watches over me
- I show up every day expecting something good is going to happen to me and through me

Even though I lacked the words to fully express what I felt, I knew that, for better or worse, we become what we behold. Brené Brown, the author of *Rising Strong: The Reckoning, The Rumble, The Revolution*, reminds us, "We must never forget, we are the authors of our lives. We write our own daring endings. We craft love from heartbreak, compassion from shame, grace from disappointment, courage from failure. Showing up is our power." In my remaining days, the least I could do was use my imagination to believe something good would happen to avert a senseless tragedy.

The research tracking what happens to emancipated teens found "the child welfare system to be a highway to homelessness, with 20 percent of those aging-out of care becoming homeless the moment they emancipate at eighteen. The struggle to find permanent, affordable, and stable housing is real." Advocates employed by The Children's Defense Fund believe, "Once in foster care, the system too often fails to provide children with stability, too many 'age out' of foster care without a permanent family. Children left with no permanent family or connection with caring adults have no one to turn to for social, emotional, or financial support and face numerous barriers as they struggle to become self-sufficient adults." A report published by the California Community Colleges Student Mental Health Program shined a light on challenges emancipated teens face as they age-out or decide to leave the system to pursue self-sufficiency and independence.

- Only 50 percent graduate from high school
- Of that number, only 20 percent gain admission to college and institutions of higher learning
- Less than 10 percent of those admitted obtain a degree

The loss of life and unfulfilled potential reflected by these numbers, while disheartening, inspired me to do something with my life. I viewed education as a pipeline to help me fulfill the basic needs of every human being identified by Psychologist Abraham Maslow in his *Hierarchy of Needs*.

As a dreamer, I had every reason to believe I could elevate from a position of surviving to thriving by becoming the person I was born to be. But the decision to terminate placement in the group home complicated my dream.

MASLOW'S HIERARCHY OF NEEDS

Needs for Self-Actualization: to be
and do that which the person was "born to do"

Needs for Esteem: self-respect
and respect from others

**Needs for Love, Affection and
Belongingness:** friendship,intimacy, family

Safety Needs: physical safety, economic safety

Physiological Needs: oxygen, food, water,
and a relatively constant body temperature

About two weeks prior to my departure, the house parent invited me into her office again. I immediately assumed a blessing of some sort was forthcoming for not ratting her out. But I received a message exceeding my wildest dreams. The house parent told me 'When you turn eighteen, you will be moving in with the owners of the group home." I accepted the invitation with a nod of approval while reigning in the impulse to jump up and down, shout, and holler because of answered prayers.

The transition to the owner's home occurred while my roommates were at school, to minimize emotional outbursts and dramatic scenes that often occur with termination of placements and relocation efforts. During the ride, the owners bombarded me with questions, which made me feel like a criminal released from a detention facility or, at best, a job applicant. OMG!

The truth of the matter is this, I knew the owners, and they knew me, but our knowing rested on superficial interactions during my two-year stay at the group home. The superficiality created a relational divide that prompted us to acknowledge we were operating at a deficit when it came to transparency and trust.

Our relationship, while amicable, suffered its fair share of difficult conversations about dating partners, my inner circle, my part-time job, driving privileges, church attendance, and college education. Most of the time, I humbled myself by adhering to their expectations. I didn't want to lose what I needed most: empathetic and caring people in my life.

But I refused to cede ground on the path I would take to rise above my circumstances. I explored what I wanted to be when I grew up. I asserted my right to decide how my future would unfold. My actions led to a cease-fire on conversations about college and freed me to pursue enrollment in criminal justice, psychology, and sociology courses, fields of study that would never run dry for lack of clients.

Despite all of the crap I went through, I focused on becoming the person I was born to be—an uplifter, encourager, pillar of faith, leader, and teacher. While continuing to work part-time, I earned a degree in the administration of justice and years later earned a bachelor's degree in criminal justice and a Juris Doctorate in Law.

By adhering to the heart-centered approach for daily living shared in Chapter 7, I beat the odds that devoured the dreams of so many peers. I would be dishonest if I downplayed the role of faith and belief in facilitating better outcomes. I know faith and belief kept the flames of *Hope, Endurance, Ambition, Resilience,* and *Truth* burning bright in my life.

Notes

CHAPTER 12

Chasing Visions and Dreams

"The future belongs to those who believe in the beauty of their dreams."

—FIRST LADY ELEANOR ROOSEVELT

I'D LOVE TO OPEN THIS chapter by saying I mastered the art of bringing all my dreams to life, but I did not. Years passed before I learned to live in the overflow of my dreams, hopes, and aspirations. Even though it's common to hit a bump or two on the way to fulfilling a dream, on more than one occasion I discovered dreams run out of steam when the heart, mind, body, soul, and spirit of the dreamer are out of alignment. When I cast my cares about the shame birthed by sexual violence onto the shoulders of the Good Shepherd, I did so without realizing I needed to remain an active participant in the healing and recovery process.

While focused on surviving and getting ahead by working part-time and attending college, I downplayed the importance of delving into mental health issues associated with my brush with trauma. Naïveté led me to believe I could experience freedom of expression, the gist of my dream at eighteen, by shoving negative feelings aside. But my false sense of security disappeared when I realized the passage of time does not produce healing. I learned the hard way what professionals in treatment and recovery programs already know: *When we deny any part of ourselves, we hold ourselves back from experiencing the fullness of life. Being in denial about our fears, traumas and pain means we cut off entire parts of ourselves.*

To a casual observer or onlooker, I appeared functional, stable, and strong. But my soul, consisting of my mind, thoughts, will, and emotions, became a landfill for dumping negative emotions, unresolved anger, and painful memories. I unwittingly became a co-conspirator, aiding and abetting the presence of trauma in my days and nights. The refusal to embrace self-care practices created a breeding ground for living a double life. I did so by creating space for the growth of learned hypocrisy.

A hypocrite is someone who pretends to hold beliefs, feelings, and opinions they do not. Learned hypocrisy is like learned helplessness, which occurs when someone repeatedly experiences a stressful situation and starts to believe they are unable to control or change the outcome, so they do not try, even when opportunities for change become available.

Learned hypocrisy made it appear that I held certain beliefs, feelings, and opinions that I did not. The persistence of ignorance about my family tree led me to veer away from cultivating meaningful and supportive relationships with workplace colleagues and college classmates. I never figured out how to navigate the getting-to-know-you phase without revealing ignorance of my family tree. My actions communicated the following belief: *I am not worthy of love because I do not have a relationship with my biological family.*

As the bearer of secrets rooted in fear of rejection, I bypassed the opportunity to cultivate relationships in exchange for spending excessive amounts of time alone. I shuttered budding friendships that carried the risk of revealing secrets I preferred to keep. My actions communicated the following belief: *As an imposter, I lack the self-esteem to connect with people based on transparency, vulnerability, and trust.*

The thought of being judged for showing up with a history in foster care and exposure to sexual violence convinced me to keep potential suitors at arm's length. Learned hypocrisy kept me from opening my heart to love and romance by reminding me of imperfections that made me unfit for intimacy as damaged goods. My actions also expressed a belief that people are not trustworthy, empathetic, or understanding.

I lived as a lone ranger for years because learned hypocrisy made perfection the standard for relationship building. A standard that robbed me, like learned helplessness, of the confidence to give love a try. By suppressing my emotions and running into the arms of learned hypocrisy, I unknowingly created fodder for becoming a victim of circumstances.

The false impressions conveyed by my actions betrayed the beliefs, feelings, and opinions I held. When I grew tired of living a double life, I paused to reflect on the impact of my decision to forego self-care by working with the Good Shepherd watching over me. I caught a glimpse of an emotionally disfigured girl entangled in a web of shame, perfectionism, and numbing behavior. That girl was me. I learned another lesson the hard way: *Denial might feel easier at first. Ignorance is bliss, however, we come to learn that we can't run from our feelings and trying to hide from them only tightens their grip on us.* Now I understood the meaning of the Serenity Prayer. The anger flowing from realization that I would never get free by running from reality led to a come-to-Jesus moment.

I set out to resolve the emotional wounds hindering freedom of expression and authenticity by seeking professional help. The real talk and mutual expectations governing our relationship created an ideal setting for dissecting and distancing myself from the adverse effects of shame, perfectionism, and numbing. I made a commitment to mend the rift between my heart, mind, body, soul, and spirit. With time, I bid farewell to the culprits eating me alive from the inside out: unexpressed anger, self-blame, denial, indifference, procrastination, and self-condemnation.

Dismantling the web of dysfunction was no easy feat. By meditating on scripture, praying, and turning from my wretched ways,

I eventually overcame addiction to learned hypocrisy. I experienced progressive healing from sexual violence by meditating on scripture to replace thoughts, attitudes, and beliefs that did not line up with my identity as a fearfully and wonderfully made child of God. The occasional feelings of shame flowing from the loss of kinship and family dissipated when I released myself from the burden of bearing responsibility for what happened.

I overcame perfectionism by learning to enjoy the journey of living rather than fixating on the outcome or destination. I discovered joy in cultivating supportive and meaningful connections with co-workers and classmates based on mutual interests and hobbies. I also embraced my sense of humor, love of comedy, and willingness to laugh at myself for missing the self-care off-ramp.

I even forged a better relationship with myself by learning to follow hunches and intuition arising from the inner witness that emerged during the healing process to confirm, "The future belongs to those who believe in the beauty of their dreams."

Rolling out with my heart, mind, body, soul, and spirit in alignment produced a much smoother ride than the senseless journey offered by anger, blame, denial, indifference, procrastination, and self-condemnation. In the process, I bridged the gap between who the Bible says I am and how I showed up. It's hard to describe what I felt, but rolling out with a unified body capable of fielding the curveballs of life felt so much better than offering bits, pieces, and fragments of myself to the world.

Bridging the gap allowed me to achieve a small, but life-changing, dream of reclaiming freedom of expression, the true source of wealth and health. I discovered that wholeness and healing are key to exercising agency, fulfilling dreams, and building heart-centered relationships at home, school, work, and with yourself.

After bridging the gap, I decided to make navigating the runway of healing and self-care a part of my life. My decision sprung in part from the realization that neither fame, fortune, nor education

could deliver freedom from wretched memories. More important-
ly, I learned the hard way that we pay a heavy price when we aid
and abet the presence of trauma in our life. I am eternally grateful
for the epiphany that led me to see that it is never too late to begin
again and partner with the Good Shepherd to experience healing
and wholeness.

Notes

CHAPTER 13

You Can Make It If You Try!

"Nothing beats a failure but a try."

—R. J. SMITH

*E*VEN THOUGH I SPENT THE better part of my life chasing a dream, I never pretended to be anything but me. As a survivor of trauma and sexual violence, I never stopped dreaming of living a life free of collateral damage produced by anger, shame, pain, resentment, and regret. My dreams might appear insignificant, but the fulfillment of each one moved me one step closer to becoming the change I wanted to see in the world.

As a teen, I responded to the call to explore issues most teens could care less about, issues that drew me in, tugging at my heart like a magnet. I wanted to know how to create order out of chaos, is there an art to finding the silver lining in negative situations?, how can I get to the other side of midnight when everything seems dark?, and how do you end a relationship with a stubborn partner like trauma?

I started sifting through memories arising from my time in foster care. My actions arose from a desire to get a handle on the larger themes at work in life. In time, this is what I discovered:

- Bad things happen to good people.
- Abuse of any kind constitutes an invasion of privacy, restricting freedom of expression.
- Trauma infiltrates the life of unsuspecting and willing hosts, until challenged by a swift and persistent kick in the butt.
- Adversity is an equal opportunity employer.
- Forgiveness and healing go hand in hand; you cannot have one without the other.
- Trouble does not last always.

Armed with this information, I set out to discover ways to create order out of chaos, find silver linings, infuse light into darkness, and recover the love, joy, and peace devoured by trauma. My plan, after figuring everything out, involved paying it forward to encourage, uplift, and support others in the healing and recovery process. But my plan remained a plan and never launched because I did not know how to use my voice to bring my dream to fruition.

While conducting research for this book, I found an article that expressed the essence of my desire. If I could roll back the hands of time to make the article available to myself as a teen, the author's words would function as wind beneath my wings. Even though I lacked the voice and support to pull off my dream as envisioned back in the day, I'm picking up where I left off to encourage, uplift, and support women and girls in the healing and recovery process.

Jennifer Gamble Theard, M.Ed., and historian with the Association for the Study of African American Life and History, in discussing the significance of the North Star for African Americans said, "The North Star, an anchor of the northern sky, is as real as it is inspirational, and as spiritual as it is celestial, to those who follow it to determine direction as it glows brightly to guide and lead toward a purposeful destination." The article addresses how and why the North Star gained so much significance in the life of African Americans:

When enslaved people in the southern United States sought freedom from those who held them as captives, they devised ways to escape. As they fled from bondage, they looked in the night sky to give them direction of where to connect to the Underground Railroad headed to the northern United States and Canada. It was the constant guidance of the North Star that gave them the starting point and continuous connections on the journey northward.

One of the most famous and successful guides and conductors of the Underground Railroad was Harriet Tubman. Once enslaved, she mastered the navigation skills of following the North Star, the God given glowing light that enabled her to help others seek freedom in the north.

The article concludes with a call to action[3] that I believe is fitting and relevant to the space we share as author and reader,

As we look within ourselves, we can seek our own internal compass that can guide us. We can discover and develop the gifts that we already have that can help us move forward as individuals and as a community.

Ms. Thread's call to action extends an invitation to women and girls who feel enslaved by their current situation to take a second look at their lives to recover everything devoured and stolen by trauma. We live in a day and time where the need for external validation and permission to become who we were born to be no longer exists. If you hold a vision for your life that meets your expectations, you should put a ring on it, make a commitment to wedding your best life ever, and escort yourself down the aisle to the desires of your heart.

---

3 An exhortation or stimulus to do something to achieve an aim or deal with a problem.

The call to seek your own internal compass as a guide requires opening your eyes to see opportunities in your midst. Patterns begin to emerge, and useful information appears amid daily routines when you set aside time to mine your life for the presence of extraordinary gifts and talents and the treasure that lies within.

For adolescents and teens, mining your life might involve identifying your loves and passions, or putting a ring on issues, topics, or interest that ignite a fire and inspire you. For readers seeking to improve their quality of life through a career or relationship change, or a business launch, mining your life for the treasure that lies within might entail sifting through the pieces of an unfulfilled dream to discern insight, wisdom, and lessons learned for future use.

Responding to the call to action requires humility to see yourself as you really are. It also requires belief in the existence of grace to begin again in the face of failure, disappointment, or squandered opportunities. Grace is defined as unmerited favor and blessing, a gift we cannot earn no matter how hard we try. Common grace is God's gift to everyone. It is the reason we enjoy the blessings of life, provision, and abundance. Grace allows us to flourish in unexpected ways each day.

Living life according to the ebb and flow of grace requires a change in perspective. In *The Message Bible*, the third chapter of the Book of Proverbs, verse 5, offers the following advice, "Trust God from the bottom of your heart; don't try to figure out everything on your own. Listen for God's voice in everything you do, everywhere you go; he's the one who will keep you on track." The wisdom flowing from this passage is key to creating order out of chaos and finding the silver lining when confronted with a negative situation or disappointing outcome.

If you are reading this book, you possess something special to light up a room, shift the atmosphere, and make a difference in the world. As you embrace who you are from God's perspective, everything changes. Neither you nor your situation can withstand the moments of lift and elevation that arise as you declare, "I am fearfully and wonderfully made."

While your current situation may leave you asking the same question I posed as a teen, How can I get to the other side of midnight when everything seems dark?, you get to the other side by letting your light shine for all to see, no matter what. The fifth chapter of the Book of Matthew, verses 14-16, as recorded in *The Voice*, offers an encouraging word of support in this area, "And you, beloved, are the light of the world. A city built on a hilltop cannot be hidden. Similarly, it would be silly to light a lamp and then hide it under a bowl. When someone lights a lamp, she puts it on a table, a desk, or a chair, and the light illumines the entire house. You are like that illuminating light. Let your light shine everywhere you go." Getting to the other side requires showing up, even if the odds of achieving what you are striving for are slim.

To discover and develop gifts and talents you already possess, you must end your relationship with trauma. This requires a conscious decision to refrain from behaviors, relationships, and habits that extend the lifecycle of what's eating you alive. Scientific experiments explaining why oil and water do not mix reveal why trafficking in dysfunction, toxic relationships, and numbing behavior never turns out for your good.

Letting go represents a rite of passage and golden opportunity to design a life tethered to the longings of your heart and spirit, rather than the collateral damage produced by trauma. Stepping up to step out on trauma creates space for taking the lead and positioning yourself to experience better outcomes in every area of life.

If my reference to oil and water does not resonate with you, fear not, you can find wisdom for calling it quits in the third chapter of the Book of Ecclesiastes, verse 3 (CEV), which says, "There is a time to kill and a time to heal. There is a time to destroy and a time to build." With regard to trauma, it's time to kill and destroy a predator devouring and emotionally disfiguring women and girls.

Once done, healing and building can occur to set women and girls free to receive the blessing recorded in the *Contemporary Bible*, in the twenty-ninth chapter of the Book of Jeremiah, verse 11, which says, "I will bless you with a future filled with hope—a future of success, not of suffering."

I discovered through trial and error and by forever leaning into the Bible, how to create order out of chaos, detect silver linings, infuse light into darkness, and recover the love, joy, and peace devoured by trauma by responding to a call. Life challenged me, despite my history with foster care, sexual violence, separation anxiety, survivor's guilt, isolation, and trauma, to step forward and become the designer, architect, and builder of my life.

For everyone reading this book, the challenge to build a life of significance remains the same and does not discriminate or come with an expiration date. Now is the time to step forward and become the designer, architect, and builder of your life, no matter what it looks like, no matter what you experienced in the past. It is time to mend the fragments of your life and unveil yourself as a gift to the world.

Even though there are an infinite number of ways to discover who you were born to be, Jim Rohn, entrepreneur, author, and motivational speaker said, "Formal education will make you a living; self-education will make you a fortune." My life and times reveal self-mastery and self-literacy are key to living your best life ever.

In Chapter 7, I shared an acrostic that served as a practical tool for making sense out of the ever-changing landscape of my life. The acrostic provided a way to create space for living with HEART— Hope, Endurance, Ambition, Resilience, and Truth—which is essential for growing in self-mastery and self-literacy. You might want to pause and refer to Chapter 7, page 44, to refresh your memory before moving on.

The options proposed thus far for cultivating and tending to the inner landscape of your life include first, creating positive affirmations, second, creating an acrostic using the word HEART or another word that resonates with you, and three, creating an internal compass and blueprint to order your steps. Whichever option you choose, let your heart be your guide. Paying attention to the longings of the heart will give you courage to try new things, step out of confined spaces created by trauma, and allow you to experience transformation from the inside out.

As an assemblage of souls well acquainted with the language of separation, severance, and loss, it's time to learn a new language and use our voices to promote whole-hearted living. In creating positive affirmations, an acrostic, or internal compass, consider using language that creates a firm foundation for rooting and grounding you in focused, intentional, and purposeful living. Use the power of your words and voice to keep you faithful, inspired, and fired up about living your best life.

As you move forward, it's important to submit your creations to the ebb and flow and outworking of time and season. The third chapter of the Book of Ecclesiastes affirms there is a right time for everything, and everything in life will happen at the right time. Whenever doubt about the fulfillment of a vision or dream arises, or you begin to fret over the delayed arrival at a destination set by your internal compass, know that the One who promised to bless you in Jeremiah 29:11 is the same One who keeps watch over the manifestation of positive affirmations, acrostics, and travel plans. As you surrender your visions, dreams, and travel plans to the creator of Heaven and Earth, you are positioning yourself to reclaim your true and authentic self and become the change you want to see in the world.

If you happen to be like me and place the needs of others ahead of yourself, I encourage you to set aside uninterrupted time to do the inner work to break free from whatever stands in the way of your ascension to greatness and better days. Whatever you desire in the way of transformation, transition, and change, you can make it if you try!

Notes

CHAPTER 14

You've Got Gifts, Talents, and Skills

"We must use what we have to invent what we desire."

—ADRIENNE RICH

BEFORE I KNEW WHAT I wanted to do with my life, I drifted into relationships, picked up habits, and frequented places that delayed my ascension to greatness. I moved about oblivious and unattuned to my gifts, talents, and skills. During this period, I adopted the name *Stumbelina* to capture what it felt like to live without purpose or meaning. I stumbled into pot dens to smoke weed with my peers. In community college, I stumbled into classes that were not a good fit. These experiences strengthened my resolve to figure out what I wanted to be when I grew up, anything but a dime piece, groupie, or college dropout.

For the mature reading audience, what I am about to share may seem like common sense, but I would be remiss if I did not address the importance of gifts, skills, and talents in helping women and girls become who they were born to be. People use the terms interchangeably, but they are not the same. Each has a different meaning, and originates from a different source. So, before moving on, I'd like to highlight the difference for those who might benefit from this information, which you might also find helpful in creating positive affirmations, an acrostic, or internal compass.

What Is a Gift or Gifts?

According to Kerry Connelly, the author of *Pause: Making Time to Walk with God,*

> Each of us has been lovingly crafted with the Artisan's hand; infused with a set of desires, skills, and affinities as unique in combination and description as our very own DNA.

Dictionary.com defines a gift as a special ability, capacity, or natural endowment we are born with. Even though we cannot acquire gifts through practice, work, or education, we can enhance their presence, effectiveness, and impact through one or more of the afore-mentioned activities. The mystique associated with gifts begins to fade when we pay attention to the gift holders in our midst. The mystique all but disappears as we open our hearts to receive the truth—there are life-changing and generative gifts inside of you and me.

Even though gifts are not visible to the human eye, it is hard to ignore or deny the benefits flowing from their operation. My experience reveals that gift holders, with the greatest of ease, no matter where they are, consistently elevate, strengthen, and uplift people, places, and causes. Everything they touch seems to get better. I have observed the benefits flowing from the heart, mind, hands, and feet of gift holders in the following places: families, places of employment, romantic relationships, friendships, business partnerships, places of worship, school settings, and community-based organizations serving disadvantaged populations.

People often use terms like exceptional, extraordinary, and inspirational to describe the enduring and transformative contributions of a gift holder. Indelible impact is an over-used but apt phrase to describe how we feel after spending time with a gift-holder.

If you are wondering, *Do I have a gift?*, the answer is *Yes*. You can discover your gifts by asking questions like:

- What am I passionate about?
- What energizes me?
- What do I enjoy doing so much I lose track of time?

You can also seek the opinions of others by asking:

- What do my coworkers, colleagues, family, and friends think I'm good at?
- Do people admire and recognize me for my work or volunteer service?
- Has anyone told me that I am gifted in some area?

The answers might offer clues for exploring career or educational paths for becoming the person you were born to be. For the mature audience, the answers might serve as a catalyst for exploring a career change, encore career, or fulfillment of a long-held dream.

Whatever you come up with, don't be like me. For years, I lived my life under the influence of a scarcity mentality. I turned into a hoarder. I hoarded many things—my time, my money, leftover food, throw-away magazines, Chinese fortune cookies, unopened gifts, my heart, my mind, my gifts, talents, skills, and my dream of living a better life. My penchant for conservation and delayed gratification almost caused me to miss the opportunity of a lifetime, a college education.

Everything changed when I decided to accept and make use of my gifts. After trashing and burning my honorary degree in denial and resistance to change, I did what I needed to do in order to become who I was born to be: an uplifter, encourager, pillar of faith, leader, and teacher.

What Is a Talent?

Talents are mental strengths that are useful to a personal pursuit, art, profession, activity, or task. Talents include innate abilities that come to a person naturally and are enhanced through learning, personal development, and disciplined practice. The following list, while not exhaustive, offers examples of talents.

- Acting
- Comedy
- Dancing
- Entrepreneurialism
- Graphic design
- Humor
- Leadership
- Magic
- Math
- Money management
- Organization
- Painting
- Playing an instrument
- Pottery
- Public speaking
- Singing
- Sporting talents
- Storytelling
- Strategic thinking
- Teaching
- Teamwork
- Woodwork
- Writing

What Is a Skill?

There are diverse skills ranging from analytical, leadership, management, professional, organizational, and project management to life skills. Irrespective of the area, a skill is demonstrated by the ability to complete a task reasonably well with expertise and proficiency. A combination of practice, work experience, and education contribute to the acquisition of skills. Below is a brief list of soft skills known to positively influence the workplace and family.

- Time management and organization
- Flexibility and creativity
- Problem-solving and critical thinking
- Excellent communication
- Collaboration and teamwork

If you have reached a state of boredom and are asking, What's the big idea behind learning about gifts, skills, and talents?, I get it and totally understand. But in keeping with the theme that we are responsible for discovering who we are, we must identify our gifts, hone our natural talents, and acquire skills to create a life mission and purpose.

According to William Damon, author of *Noble Purpose, The Joy of Living a Meaningful Life*, "Purpose is a key part of our personal search for meaning, but it also has an external quality, a desire to make a difference in the world, to contribute to matters beyond our own self-interest. Purpose creates resiliency, even in the face of the most terrible events."

Identifying your gifts, honing your talents, and acquiring skills also represents a necessary rite of passage[4] for making sense of your life. According to Brené Brown, author of *The Gifts of Imperfection*, "Whether

---

4 A ritual, event, or experience that marks or constitutes a major milestone or change in a person's life.

we're overcoming adversity, surviving trauma, or dealing with stress and anxiety, having a sense of purpose, meaning, and perspective in our lives allows us to develop understanding and move forward."

The discovery of your life purpose and mission ranks high on the list of activities required to make yourself known and amplify your voice in everyday life. The dual purpose of making sense of your life while making a difference in the world appears to be a common thread running through the lives of people with lived experience in foster care. Every time I cross paths with a kindred spirit, I know I am in the presence of someone to be reckoned with. Individually and collectively, in a mysterious way, we are on assignment to make the world a better place through our presence, service, and good works.

It is never too soon or too late to begin crafting a life mission and purpose statement. You can do so by answering a couple of questions if you're just starting out, or want to update the one you have:

- Who do you believe you were born to be?
- What do you want to do with your life?
- What are you good at?
- What are your gifts, talents, and skills?
- Is there are recurring theme or passion that continues to come up in your life?
- Is there a childhood dream you would like to pursue?
- What positive impact do you want to have on your family, workplace, or community?
- Are you willing to do what it takes to unveil yourself as a gift to the world?

As you reflect on these questions and commit your thoughts to paper or an electronic device, think about opportunities that will engage your heart, mind, body, soul, and spirit. If you like your answers and want to put a ring on it, you might consider one or more of the following activities:

- Create a vision board or attend a workshop to learn how to create one.
- Keep a journal to capture information revealed during times of reflection.
- Place a whiteboard in your home office or other area to keep your life mission and purpose before you.
- Develop a business plan if you're interested in starting a business.

Deena Saunders-Green, an experienced and exceptional contributor to advancing better outcomes for people with lived experience in foster care, created and published the *Transitional Age Youth Entrepreneurs Workbook* for anyone interested in starting a business. However, it was specifically created to help business-minded young adults affected by foster care, the juvenile justice system, or children's mental health services.

Whatever you decide, don't forget to share your life mission and purpose with a best friend, significant other, trusted family member, classmate, or colleague. Surround yourself with a great cloud of witnesses to support and encourage you while fulfilling your life mission and purpose.

I have included several resources to assist with identifying your gifts, honing your talents, and enhancing your knowledge of resources available to assist with the acquisition of skills. The first resource, *The Gift of Standout*, is free. As someone who completed the assessment twice to gain insight prior to making a career shift, I found the complimentary fourteen-page report to be spot-on and credible. The second resource, the CliftonStrengths assessments will help identify your natural talents, so you can perform better in the workplace, build stronger relationships, and achieve personal growth.

A link to websites maintained by the U. S. Bureau of Labor Statistics profiling more than 324 occupations and a searchable database designed specifically for students of more than sixty occupations based on their interest are also included.

I hope these resources are helpful and inspire a desire for deeper learning about who you are.

RESOURCES TO AID IN THE DISCOVERY OF GIFTS, TALENTS, AND SKILLS

ONLINE TOOLS

1.) In response to the COVID-19 global health crisis, Marcus Buckingham, ADP®, and Harvard Business Publishing have created The Gift of StandOut®, which includes a Complimentary StandOut® strengths assessment and a fourteen-page detailed report describing your greatest sources of strength and contribution.

2.) CliftonStrengths Assessments
StrengthsFinder 2.0—Discover your Clifton Strengths
https://store.gallup.com/c/en-us/assessments

3.) Live Your Best Life Using Your Strengths
https://www.gallup.com/cliftonstrengths/en/home.aspx

CAREER INFORMATION FOR STUDENTS

- Allows students to search more than sixty occupations based on their interests
- https://www.bls.gov/k12/students/careers/career-exploration.htm
- The Occupational Outlook Handbook (OOH) generated by the U.S. Bureau of Labor Statistics provides information for 324 occupations in the public and private sectors.
- https://www.bls.gov/ooh/home.htm

RECOMMENDED READING

- *StrengthsFinder 2.0—Discover your CliftonStrengths*, Gallup and Tom Rath, Gallop Press, 2017.
- *Noble Purpose—The Journey of Living a Meaningful Life*, William Damon, Templeton Fountain Press, 2003.
- *Love + Work: How to Find What You Love, Love What You Do, and Do It for The Rest of Your Life*, Marcus Buckingham, Harvard Business Review Press, 2022.
- *Transitional Age Youth Entrepreneurs Workbook*, Deena Saunders-Green, Green Pines Media, 2017.

Notes

CHAPTER 15

Look to The Stars

WHILE NAVIGATING THE SEASONS OF life in foster care, it never dawned on me to look to the stars, celestial or otherwise, for inspiration, motivation, or guidance. While conducting research for this project, I uncovered information about females, past and present, who share a history of lived experience in foster or kinship care. Chris Chmielewski, Creator, Owner, and Editor of *Foster Focus Magazine*, the nation's only magazine devoted to foster care, assembled the best-known source of information about public and historical figures, athletes, musicians, artists, sports professionals, and entertainers with lived experience.

I have included an abbreviated profile of five kindred spirits met along the way to shine a light on women who have walked in our shoes.

SIMONE BILES—GYMNAST/OLYMPIAN/PRESIDENTIAL MEDAL OF FREEDOM RECIPIENT
Kinship Care/Adopted
Simone Biles is the youngest person to ever receive the Presidential Medal of Freedom and is also the most decorated gymnast of all time.

As an American artistic gymnast, she is well known for her individual gold medal at the 2016 Olympic Games, held in Brazil. She is an artistic gymnast and typically excels at the all-round, floor, and vault gymnastics. Simone Biles has been a world champion in all three for several years. She has won thirty-two Olympic and World Championship medals overall, making her the most-celebrated American gymnast and the most-decorated gymnast ever. She has a record for the most gold medals won by an American woman at a single Olympic Games. She is only the sixth woman to win both the Olympic medal and the World Championship medal in all-round individual title.

Simone was born to Shanon Biles and Kelvin Clemons on March 14, 1997, in Columbus, Ohio. Simone's father was never a part of her life, as he struggled with addiction problems and abandoned his family. Simone's mother, Shanon, was also a victim of drug and alcohol addiction. She did not play a significant part in the raising of her children either. Simone was brought up by her maternal grandfather, Ron Biles, and his wife Nellie Cayetano Biles.

KEYSHIA COLE—SINGER
Foster Care/Kinship Care
Keyshia Cole is no stranger to overcoming adversity, as her mother's battle with drug addiction led her to give her up for adoption. Instead of letting the circumstances get her down, Keyshia Cole worked hard to make her dream of becoming an entertainer come to pass.

TIFFANY HADDISH—ACTRESS
Foster Care
Tiffany Haddish, an American comedian, is known for her unflinching candor and disarming authenticity. She shot to stardom with her no-holds-barred performance as Dina in *Girls Trip* (2017). She was named one of the 100 most influential people in the world by *Time* magazine in 2018, and *The Hollywood Reporter* listed her among the 100 most

powerful people in entertainment in both 2018 and 2019. She won a Primetime Emmy Award for hosting a *Saturday Night Live* episode (2017) and published a memoir, *The Last Black Unicorn* (2017). Haddish released the album *Black Mitzvah* in 2019, for which she won the Grammy Award for Best Comedy Album, making her the second African American woman to win this prize after Whoopi Goldberg in 1986.

Tiffany's father, an Eritrean, left the family when she was still a toddler. After her mother suffered brain damage in a car accident, she spent several years in foster care before going to live with her grandmother as a teenager. Her penchant for making her classmates laugh led her social worker to point her toward the Laugh Factory Comedy Camp, a free summer program offered by the comedy club chain Laugh Factory to teach underprivileged children how to perform stand-up comedy. The camp proved to be a transformative experience for Haddish.

ELLA FITZGERALD—SINGER
Kinship Care

Geoffrey Mark, the author of *ELLA: A Biography of the Legendary Ella Fitzgerald*, while reflecting on the singer's life said, "Ella Fitzgerald was discovered by God. She had an awful childhood… She was beaten, battered, abused, left on her own after her mother's death, with the government grabbing her and sticking her in this awful place where children were sent— far away from where she was living with her mother's companion." According to the author, whenever Ella faced a challenge, she relied on her faith, believing that if she did the right thing, if she worked hard, the outcome would work in her favor.

ANITA BAKER—SINGER
Foster Care/Adopted

In an interview with *Essence* magazine, the singer opened up about the pain she endured for years after learning her birth mother gave her up for adoption when she was a baby. Baker was thirteen years old when she learned the woman she thought was her mother was actually her foster parent. After the death of her foster mother, Anita was adopted by an aunt, who provided her with a stable environment that emphasized hard work and religion.

Like these kindred spirits, women and girls own the creative rights to determine how they turn up and show up in life. Somewhere along the way Simone, Keyshia, Tiffany, Ella, and Anita demonstrated the courage to do these things:

- Discover and use their voices
- Embrace their gifts, talents, and skills
- Make life-affirming choices
- Transform tragedy into triumph

I will never know for sure, but I believe each one cultivated the following characteristics to support their ascension to greatness:

- Ambition
- Fortitude
- Humility
- Inner strength
- Positive attitude
- Resilience
- Vision

Of all the traits, ambition trumps them all, because ambition motivates and inspires people to accomplish remarkable things.

According to Peter Economy, contributing writer with *Inc.* magazine, "Ambitious people take charge of their destiny and don't expect others to bow down to their needs. They have willpower and determination. They know where they are going and what they must do to get there. They are capable of changing and measuring up to their dreams, always watchful of the opportunities out there for those who are willing to see them and seize them." The gist of Peter's message is this: Ambitious people create tools, strategies, and tactics to turn their dreams into reality. They understand the benefit of cultivating awareness, seizing opportunities, and weathering the winds of adversity and change.

The women highlighted in this chapter did more than memorialize their vision and dream. They invested in themselves. They believed they could transcend any hurdle, hindrance, or obstacle encountered along the way. They owned their story. They demonstrated courage and resilience while en route to the fulfillment of their dreams. They wielded their magic to discover their life mission and purpose and unveiled themselves as a gift to the world.

While researching the lives of these women, I discovered a recurring theme in interviews and news articles. In addition to experiencing adversity and hardship, each one acknowledges the importance of faith and belief. Simone Biles frequently credits her faith for her success in her book, *Courage to Soar*, published by Zondervan. Keyshia Cole during an interview said, "I'm a strong believer that if you keep your faith right, you'll make sure you get what you want out of life because it's possible. I mean, anything is possible especially with God by your side." Tiffany Haddish, in reflecting on a throwback picture of herself performing a stand-up gig and the promise she made to herself years ago when she was homeless, said "I look at this picture and want to cry tears of joy for this girl. I remember that night. She was homeless, hungry, scared, and hurt. I promised her if she kept faith in God and Herself, we will get to a place where we will be housed, over fed, less hurt, and fear free."

As you and I behold these women, we realize we are more alike than different. As kindred spirits, our connection is real. There is hope, solace, and comfort in knowing we are not alone. There are seeds of greatness pulsing in our veins! We can take our place alongside these women who walked in our shoes, and replace feelings of guilt and shame with a badge of humility, honor, and grace for having made it this far. The truth of the matter is this: everybody is a star, but we must open our eyes to see who we are.

It is time to turn up and encourage one another to live with a sense of expectancy that something good is going to happen to us, and through us like it did for Simone, Keyshia, Tiffany, Ella, and Anita. It's time to turn up and look to the stars of the past, present, and future!

And if you ever pull up short in accomplishing a goal or something on your to-do list, be encouraged by the words of Truman Capote and Maya Angelou, kindred spirits with lived experience in foster and kinship care. Both knew a thing or two about putting defeat and failure in perspective.

"Failure is the condiment that gives success its flavor."

—TRUMAN CAPOTE

"You may encounter many defeats, but you must not be defeated.
In fact, it may be necessary to encounter the defeats, so you can
know who you are, what you can rise from,
how you can still come out of it."

—MAYA ANGELOU

Notes

CHAPTER 16

It's Time to Turn Up—
No More Trauma

"Appreciate where you are in your journey. Even if it is not where you want to be. Every season serves a purpose."

—MARIA SHRIVER

To KEEP TRACK OF THE ever-changing landscape of my life, like a clock wound too tight, I colored everything in shades of black and white. I neatly filed events and occurrences into categories, like life lessons, epiphanies, insights, and building blocks. On the other hand, when things did not turn out as planned, I labeled them as obstacles, hurdles, hindrances, and dream killers. By neatly filing everything away, I bypassed opportunities to revisit and explore gray areas and liminal space for insight and wisdom for future use.

A *liminal space* is the time between what was and next. It is a place of transition, a time of waiting and not knowing the future. Richard Rohr describes liminal space as, "where we are betwixt and between the familiar and the completely unknown." My own frenetic search for light at the end of the tunnel of a trauma-inducing child welfare system caused me to move at a dizzying and robotic pace, often losing sight of opportunities for growth. I never stopped long enough to breathe, let alone embrace the possibility that a thing called maybe sits between yes and no, and there is a place of repose between stop and go. All of this may sound like a riddle, but stick with me, because I'm going somewhere.

Rather than pause to master the possibilities for growth, maturity, and change associated with my own betwixt and between times, I responded to whatever I experienced with habits, tactics, strategies, and defense mechanisms pulled from an old bag of tricks. I never stopped to consider that an obstacle might be life's way of encouraging me to seek an alternative path. Or that a hurdle obstructing forward progress represented a call to open my eyes to other options. *Could the hindrance standing in my way be a signal that something better exists beyond my line of sight?* Maybe the dream killers I neatly filed away represented life's way of communicating that the best is yet to come.

Whatever the case, in bypassing the opportunity to harvest the deeper meaning of my experiences, I fell into the habit of committing senseless errors and mistakes. Years later, I discovered my repeat performances arose from behaviors programmed into memory by the adverse effects of trauma, behavior discussed in chapters one through fourteen. You often hear people offer up the following quote attributed to Albert Einstein, "Insanity is doing the same thing over and over and expecting different results." If that's the case, I'm the first to admit I lived an insane life for a very long time.

But one day I realized I was not stuck on stupid, or any of these things: stubborn, a masochist, addicted to pain and suffering, ambulating through life with an undiagnosed case of obsessive-compulsive personality disorder. And neither are you.

Researchers and mental health professionals are lining up in droves to acknowledge and talk about what I already know about the concerns plaguing you and me. When we go through trauma, our brains do not function like they normally do. The exposure to trauma deprives us of the capacity to break free of learned behaviors that block the ability of the brain to make use of gray areas and liminal space.

For lack of a better way to explain it, the crazy glue generated by trauma binds us to an unconscious and repetitive spin-cycle of pain and suffering. According to Isaac Smith, founder of Whole Wellness Therapy,

> Trauma can change the way we think, feel, and act for a long time after the initial event. For many this could mean flashbacks or nightmares, a constant feeling of being on edge, loneliness, anger, intrusive thoughts and memories, self-destructive actions, and more.

> Trauma can change your brain from the way you make decisions down to your immediate, subconscious responses to the world around you. Part of the reason it can be so hard to overcome the effects of trauma is that it infiltrates and attacks several areas of the brain at once.

> These parts are: The amygdala, which is your emotional and instinctual center; the hippocampus, which controls memory; and the prefrontal cortex, which is responsible for regulating your emotions and impulses. All three parts work together to manage stress.

> Trauma can cause your brain to remain in a state of hyper vigilance, suppressing your memory and impulse control and trapping you in a constant state of strong emotional reactivity.

My only question after sharing Isaac Smith's crash course on how trauma affects the brain, is this, *Is it any wonder you and I struggle to break free of the adverse effects of trauma, which often sabotage our suc-*

cess, when it comes to things like self-care, our relationships, the pursuit of education, and the fulfillment of our life mission and purpose?

I can't speak for anyone else, but the adverse effects of trauma wrecked my ability to see myself, other people, and life events through the lens of truth. I repeatedly tripped over emotional wounds, triggering explosions, and leaving a trail of missed opportunities, shattered dreams, and short-lived relationships behind.

The old dirty bastards (ODB) birthed by trauma mentioned in Chapter 3 subtly defined the circumference of my life. The ODBs called the shots by using a repertoire of life-draining actions and behavior. The collateral damage arising from my brush with trauma paints a picture of what a brain looks like when operating under the influence of crazy glue:

- Without consciously doing so, I found myself tethered to patterns, routines, and ruts that did not reflect my true and authentic self or serve my best interests.
- Learned dysfunctional behavior became my modus operandi overshadowing the desires of my heart.
- The rhythm of my days and nights unfolded according to synchronized routines rooted and grounded in a past that no longer served me.
- I showed up, showed out, and acted out by leaning on standard operating procedures and survival techniques not fitting for someone fearfully and wonderfully made in the image of the Creator of Heaven and Earth.

But one day grace, the unmerited favor and blessing of God appeared, bringing to life a truth acknowledged by Isaac Smith, "It might seem like trauma does irreversible damage to your brain, but that's not true. Our brains are extremely adaptable. Neuroplasticity, the brain's ability to form new connections, explains why we can rewire our brains to reverse trauma's damaging effects."

Grace supplied everything I needed to break ranks with the lesser version of myself birthed by trauma. Grace opened my eyes to see nothing, especially the ODBs, could separate me from the love of God or the Good Shepherd watching over me. I memorialized the revelation by affirming, "I am better than this! A mind is a terrible thing to waste trafficking in trauma."

I started rewiring my brain by sowing seeds of love, hope, faithfulness, and endurance into the gray areas and liminal space. I nourished what I planted with lessons learned, epiphanies, insights, and building blocks amassed over the years. I severed my connection to learned dysfunctional synchronized behaviors by converting obstacles, hurdles, hindrances, and dream killers into steppingstones for ascension to higher ground. I resuscitated and renewed my mind by keeping a journal while praying for release from the lesser version of myself.

All of this to say, I made a conscious decision to *step up* and *step out* on trauma and the ODBs she bore. Everything about my life up to this point indicated that, in the absence of a swift and persistent kick in the butt, trauma spreads like cancer to infiltrate the heart, mind, body, soul, and spirit. At its best, trauma seeks to destroy what it did not create, fearfully and wonderfully made women and men, boys, and girls, created in the likeness and image of the creator of Heaven and Earth. It also seeks to steal kill and destroy our ability to live an abundant life.

To cross over to the abundant life promised by John 10:10, (NKJV), and seize the hope and future promised by Jeremiah 29:11, we must recognize what time it is. The third chapter of Ecclesiastes offers guidance for interpreting the sign of the times. According to verses 2-3 (AMP), "There is a time to be born and a time to die, a time to plant and a time to pull out what was planted, a time to kill and a time to heal, a time to tear down and a time to build up." Let these words be your guide in responding to the following calls to action.

- Unmask, tear down, deconstruct, and uproot the adverse effects of trauma in your life.
- Stop allowing your mind to play tricks on you in broad daylight.
- Check yourself before your wreck yourself while operating under the influence of trauma.
- Seek help from a spirit-filled and spirit-led mental health professional to invite faith and belief into the healing and recovery process to break every chain, crash pity parties, and bust a move.

Don't spend another day trafficking in trauma, because a mind is a terrible thing to waste. It's time to stop playing hide and seek with self-care routines rooted in love, the most durable power in the world. It's time to *step up* and *step out* on trauma to exercise stewardship over your heart, mind, body, soul, and spirit. It's time to come full circle and harvest the seeds of greatness embedded in your DNA. The deliverables will allow you to live your best life and become an inspiration and blessing to others.

I know it's not easy, but once you *step up* and *step out*, faith and belief will supply the oxygen needed to keep the desires of your heart burning bright. By faith, we are empowered to move mountains of memories stored in the archives of our lives to the recycle bin for disposal. Matthew 17:20 says, "If you have faith like a grain of mustard seed, you will say to this mountain, 'Move from here to there,' and it will move, and nothing will be impossible for you." Receive it and believe it. It's already done! The best is yet to come!

It's time to turn up, bid farewell to the roots and shoots[5] of trauma, and declare your worth as a fearfully and wonderfully made gift to the world.

Pick up your crown wherever you laid it down. Grab your travel bag and don't forget to pack your positive affirmations, acrostic,

---

5 The main difference between a shoot and a root is that shoots are parts of the plant that grow above the ground, whereas roots are parts of the plant that grow below the ground.

internal compass, magic, and scepter. Prepare to take your rightful place and turn up for the next chapter or season of your life.

—— LIFELINES FOR FEARLESS LIVING ——

By acknowledging that trouble does not last always, we can make peace with our past. These are the lifelines and insights cast by the stories in Part III:

1. We can create space for living with heart by clinging to the truth of who we are – beautiful, powerful, and creative.

2. We can position ourselves to live our best life by refusing to show up double minded.

3. We can achieve our hopes, dreams, and aspirations by ridding ourselves of what's holding us back.

4. We can build an enduring legacy by breaking every chain limiting the full use of our gifts and talents.

5. We can ascend to greatness by embracing an unshakable commitment to our life mission and purpose.

6. We can become who we were born to be by ending the spin cycle birthed by trauma.

Notes

Epilogue: Each One, Teach One

An African proverb says, "Each one, teach one." Wikipedia indicates the proverb originated in the United States during the time of slavery, when Africans were denied education, including learning to read. Many if not most enslaved people were kept in a state of ignorance about anything beyond their immediate circumstances, which were under the control of owners, lawmakers, and authorities. When an enslaved person learned or was taught to read, it became their duty to teach someone else, spawning the phrase "Each one, teach one."

I have lived long enough to know what presents a challenge for me may not faze you. And what troubles you may be something I have already cycled through. But when you get right down to it, we need each other to survive, oddities and idiosyncrasies aside. I pray we never reach the day where we are inclined to place a do-not-resuscitate sticker on someone's life, because we are more than our setbacks, disappointments, and failures, often rooted in exposure to trauma.

My life and times reveal that people with lived experience in foster care and exposure to trauma, are often *called* without the support of immediate or extended family to complete one of the most courageous journeys in life: discovering and fulfilling their life mission and purpose. But the reflections, epiphanies, insights, and words of wisdom shared throughout this book confirm what I know to be true. We can use our divinity, creativity, and power to bring about the future we desire.

As I bring this book to a close, I offer these words of encouragement to support our continued growth, maturity, and ascension to greatness:

> You and I are more than enough and possess everything we need to experience positive life change. We owe it to ourselves to turn up and unveil ourselves as a gift to the world, even when faced with challenging odds.

We cannot turn a deaf ear to the call to get on with living life without traumatizing ourselves all over again. But getting on requires preparation for the long haul, like a marathon runner. Our success in rising above our past will require the intentional and strategic use of our gifts, talents, and skills. Using what we have is mandatory, not optional. I have lived long enough to know life will not dispatch a search and rescue party to help us get over setbacks and challenges encountered along the way. It is futile to expect others to meet our needs. The most practical option for experiencing positive life change involves mining our lives for the treasure that lies within.

But I also know from experience that when we reach the end of ourselves and struggle to place one foot in front of the other, the God who infuses us with a set of desires, skills, and affinities as unique in combination and description as our very own DNA, will intervene to do what we cannot do for ourselves and will make a way out of no way.

That's what I experienced in chapter ten when I received the unexpected invitation to move in with the owners of the group home for girls as the child welfare agency prepared to kick me to the curb. In the words of Anne Lamott, "I do not understand the mystery of grace—only that it meets us where we are but does not leave us where it found us."

Grace is defined as unmerited favor and blessing, a gift we cannot earn, no matter how hard we try. Many, if not all of the things we enjoy on a day-to-day basis are a result of nothing more and nothing less than the grace of God. Common grace is God's gift to everyone. It is the reason we enjoy the blessings of life, provision, and abundance.[6] Grace allows us to flourish in unexpected ways each day.

Author Max Lucado travels back in time, then makes a bee-line to the present in *Grace, More Than We Deserve, Greater Than We Imagine*, to demonstrate how grace appears in our lives. The touch and feel of grace are real because:

- Grace comes after you.
- Grace rewires you.
- Grace calls you to change and supplies the power to pull it off.

The only prerequisite to receiving the support, strength, and protection offered by grace is faith. John Stott said, "Faith's only function is to receive what grace offers." I do not know about you, but I'm standing with my arms open, ready to receive whatever grace sends my way. Grace changes lives!

I opened this book with a disclaimer indicating this is not a bible study or a deep dive into scripture, but a memoir shared to demonstrate how four scriptures changed my life from the inside out. But I'm going to end where I started by referring to the twenty-ninth chapter of the Book of Jeremiah, verse 11 (NIV), which says "For I know the plans I have for you, plans to prosper you and not to harm you, plans to give you hope and a future."

Even if you have never owned a bible or attended church, consider setting aside time to reflect on the meaning of this passage. Listen for guidance and reflect upon what is true and right for you as you harvest the meaning of your life experiences. Sometimes

---

6 What Is the Difference Between Common Grace and Saving Grace? https://www. christiantoday.com/article/what-is-the-difference-between-common-grace-and-saving-grace/104278.htm

embracing a vision larger than you can see is key to experiencing breakthrough. Never underestimate the power of grace to meet you where you are and place you on a path to turn up and unveil yourself as a gift to the world.

If you keep the faith, keep on keeping on, and embrace the call to get on with living life, you will discover the truth that sets you free—free from every detour, defeat, deception, delusion, disappointment, and distortion birthed by trauma.

May grace meet you where you are and supply your every need.

Lady D

Notes

The websites referenced in this book were live and correct at the time of publication but may be subject to change.

Dedication
• Pressfield, Steven. *The War of Art: Break Through the Blocks and Win Your Inner Creative Battles,* Warner Books Edition (2002).

Special Message from the Author
• Lived experience is defined as personal knowledge about a social issue like domestic violence, homelessness, addiction, or foster care, gained through direct, first-hand involvement, rather than representations constructed by other people. It is also defined as the experiences of people on whom a social issue or combination of issues has had a direct impact. Google Quick Answer.
• Brown, Brené. Shame vs. Guilt
  https://brenebrown.com/articles/2013/01/15/shame-v-guilt/
• Children's Law Center of California
  https://www.clccal.org/resources/foster-care-facts/

Introduction
• Gores, Kelly Noonan. *Heal: Discover Your Unlimited Potential and Awaken the Powerful Healer,* Atria Books/Beyond Words; 1st Edition, October 22, 2019.

Chapter 1
• Lorde, Audre. *Sister Outsider: Essays and Speeches,* Crossing Press; Reprint edition, August 1, 2007.
• What Is the #MeToo Movement?
  https://www.verywellmind.com/what-is-the-metoo-movement-4774817
• MeToo Movement
  https://metoomvmt.org/
• Tarana Burke
  https://www.taranaburke.com/

- Girls in Foster Care - A Vulnerable and High-Risk Group. Elizabeth B. Dowell, PhD, RN, CRNP; Deborah J. Cavanaugh, MA, MHC; Ann W. Burgess, DNSc, RN, FAAN; Robert A. Prentky, PhD. *MCN, The American Journal of Maternal/Child Nursing*: May 2009 - Volume 34 - Issue 3 - p 172-178 doi: 10.1097/01.NMC.0000351705.43384.2a.
- Herman Law—A Voice for Victims of Sexual Abuse https://hermanlaw.com/
- DNA Proves Foster Father Raped, Impregnated Young Girl, But Court System Kept Her Living There https://www.wpxi.com/news/investigates/dna-proves-foster-father-raped-impregnated-young-girl-court-system-kept-her-living-there/HIM6NAQHAVFFLM6Z3A5ELTIGQY/
- Foster Dad Who Impregnated Girl Twice While Wife Slept in Same Bed Is Jailed https://metro.co.uk/2016/06/11/foster-dad-who-impregnated-girl-twice-while-wife-slept-in-same-bed-is-jailed-5937980/
- Lawsuit: Woman Alleges Foster Brother Impregnated Her, LA County Case Worker Arranged Abortion https://abc7.com/dcfs-lawsuit-sexual-abuse-child/10904099/
- Arrien, Angeles. *The Second Half of Life: Opening the Eight Gates of Wisdom*, Sounds True, 2006.

Chapter 2

- Substance Abuse and Mental Health Services Administration. *SAMHSA's "Concept of Trauma and Guidance for a Trauma-Informed Approach."* HHS Publication No. (SMA) 14-4884. Rockville, MD: Substance Abuse and Mental Health Services Administration, 2014.
- Hall, M., & Hall, J. (2011). "The long-term effects of childhood sexual abuse: Counseling implications." https://www.counseling.org/docs/disaster-and-trauma_sexual-abuse/long-term-effects-of-childhood-sexual-abuse.pdf?sfvrsn=2
- Adverse Childhood Experiences https://www.cdc.gov/violenceprevention/aces/index.html

Chapter 3

- Northrup, Christiane M.D. *A Daily Dose of Women's Wisdom*, Hay House Inc., November 2017. www.drnorthrup.com.
- What Is Forgiveness? https://greatergood.berkeley.edu/topic/forgiveness/definition#what-is-forgiveness

Chapter 4
- Northrup, Christiane M.D. *A Daily Dose of Women's Wisdom*, Hay House Inc., November 2017. www.drnorthrup.com.

Chapter 5
- Did MLK Say "Our Lives Begin to End the Day We Become Silent"? https://www.snopes.com/fact-check/mlk-our-lives-begin-to-end/
- Chu, Sienna LMHC. "Inner Child Wounds: Identifying core wounds as the first step towards healing." https://www.intuitivehealingnyc.com/blog/2021/5/3/inner-child-wounds-identifying-core-wounds-as-the-first-step-towards-healing

Chapter 6
- Gordon-Reed, Annette. *On Juneteenth*. Liveright Publishing Corporation, 2021.
- Washington, Booker T. *Up From Slavery: An Autobiography*. Garden City, New York, Doubleday & Company, Inc., 1901.
- Williamson, Marianne. "Our Deepest Fear" https://www.personalgrowthcourses.net/stories/williamson.ourdeepestfear.invitation

Chapter 7
- Davis, Angela Y. *Freedom is a Constant Struggle, Ferguson, Palestine, and the Foundation of a Movement*. Haymarket Books, 2016.
- Steiner, Claude. *Emotional Literacy—Intelligence with a Heart*, Personhood Press, 2003.

Chapter 8
- Northrup, Christiane M.D. *A Daily Dose of Women's Wisdom*, Hay House Inc., November 2017. www.drnorthrup.com.
- California Department of Social Services https://www.cdss.ca.gov/inforesources/foster-care/group-homes
- Phagen-Hansel, Kim. "The Power of Story." *Fostering Families Today*, May/June 2021, page 3.

Chapter 9
- Taylor, Susan L. *Lessons in Living*, Anchor Book, 1995.
- Brown, Brené. *The Gifts of Imperfection*, 10th Anniversary Edition, Random House, 2020. Cultivating Authenticity: Letting Go of What People Think.
- Asheville Academy https://ashevilleacademy.com/

Chapter 10
- Psalms 139:13-14 New International Version
- David's Victories and Failure, Triumphs and Tragedies
  https://www.agapebiblestudy.com/charts/David's%20Victories%20
  and%20Failures.htm
- I am - Daily Affirmations
  Positive Reminders Motivation
  Monkey Taps
  https://monkeytaps.net/

Chapter 11
- Brown, Brené. *Rising Strong: The Reckoning. The Rumble. The Revolution.*
  Random House; Reprint edition, August 25, 2015.
- Proverbs 13:3 (AMP)
- The National Foster Youth Institute
  https://nfyi.org/issues/homelessness/
- The National Foster Youth Institute
  https://nfyi.org/issues/higher-education/
- Children's Defense Fund
  https://www.childrensdefense.org/policy/policy-priorities/child-
  welfare/
- Maslow's Hierarchy of Needs Explained
  https://www.thoughtco.com/maslows-hierarchy-of-needs-4582571
- Supporting Transition-Aged Foster Youth
  California Community Colleges Student Mental Health Program
  https://www.cccstudentmentalhealth.org/resource/supporting-
  transition-aged-foster-youth/

Chapter 12
- https://www.brainyquote.com/quotes/eleanor_roosevelt_100940
- How Denial Holds Us Back from Healing
  https://enlightenedsolutions.com/how-denial-holds-us-back-from-
  healing/

Chapter 13
- Theard, Jennifer Gamble M.Ed., Association for the Study of African
  American Life and History Historian, "The North Star: A symbol of
  Inspiration and Hope," *The Weekly Challenger,* January 17, 2019.
  https://theweeklychallenger.com/the-north-star-a-symbol-of-
  inspiration-and-hope/#:~:text=The%20North%20Star%
  20is%20the,lead%20toward%20a%20purposeful%20
  destination.

- Wells, Stephanie. "What Is Inner Work and How to Transform Your Life" https://thriveglobal.com/stories/what-is-inner-work-and-how-to-transform-your-life/

Chapter 14
- Connelly, Kerry. *Pause: Making Time to Walk with God*, Bright and Happy Books, 2017.
- Damon, William. *Nobel Purpose, The Joy of Living a Meaningful Life*, Templeton Foundation Press, 2003.
- Brown, Brené. *The Gifts of Imperfection*, 10th Anniversary Edition, Random House, 2020. Cultivating A Resilient Spirit: Letting Go of Numbing and Powerlessness.
- Occupational Outlook Handbook (OOH), U.S. Bureau of Labor Statistics, April 2022. https://www.bls.gov/ooh/home.htm
- Career Information for Students – U.S. Bureau of Labor Statistics https://www.bls.gov/k12/students/careers/career-exploration.htm
- StandOut® Strengths Assessment by Marcus Cunningham https://www.marcusbuckingham.com/gift-of-standout/
- CliftonStrengths Assessments https://store.gallup.com/c/en-us/assessments
- Saunders-Green, Deena. *Transitional Age Youth Entrepreneurs Workbook*, July 5, 2017, Green Pines Media.
- Examples of Skills https://examples.yourdictionary.com/examples-of-skills.html
- Examples of Talents https://simplicable.com/new/talent-examples

Chapter 15
- Chmielewski, Chris. "Famous Foster/Adopted Kids," *Foster Focus* https://www.fosterfocusmag.com/famous-foster-kids.
- Economy, Peter. "Remarkably Positive Power of Ambition." *Inc.*, May 23, 2021.
- Simone Biles https://sportsspectrum.com/sport/olympics/2018/11/05/simone-biles-relies-on-faith-as-she-continues-setting-gymnastics-world-records/
- Simone Biles Biography (Most Decorated Gymnast of All Time) https://www.thefamouspeople.com/profiles/simone-biles-32980.php
- Keyshia Cole: Anything Is Possible Especially With GOD By Your Side https://www.ulizalinks.co.ke/keyshia-cole-anything-is-possible-especially-with-god-by-your-side/

- Tiffany Haddish
  https://www.britannica.com/biography/Tiffany-Haddish
  https://en.wikipedia.org/wiki/Tiffany_Haddish
  https://www.usatoday.com/story/life/people/2019/04/25/tiffany-haddish-shares-photo-being-homeless-hungry-scared/3580644002/
- Mark, Geoffrey. *ELLA: A Biography of the Legendary Ella Fitzgerald, Ultimate Symbol*, March 1, 2018.
  https://www.foxnews.com/entertainment/ella-fitzgerald-and-marilyn-monroe-bonded-after-suffering-from-abusive-childhoods-book-claims
- Anita Baker
  https://www.essence.com/news/anita-baker-has-no-regrets/
  https://biography.jrank.org/pages/2387/Baker-Anita.html
- Economy, Peter. "Remarkably Positive Power of Ambition." *Inc.*, May 23, 2021.
  https://www.inc.com/peter-economy/the-remarkably-positive-power-of-ambition.html

Chapter 16
- https://www.inaliminalspace.org/about-us/what-is-a-liminal-space
- How Does Trauma Affect the Brain? - And What It Means for You
  https://www.wholewellnesstherapy.com/post/trauma-and-the-brain

Epilogue
- Lucado, Max. *Grace, More Than We Deserve, Grater Than We Imagine.* Thomas Nelson, 2012.

ABOUT THE AUTHOR

AS THE RECIPIENT OF THREE post-secondary degrees, Lady D excelled in the public and private sector by adhering to a simple but life-changing tenet: "Nothing is impossible when pursued in faith and belief."

She leveraged opportunities to lead, serve, and love, by delivering world-class service to a broad range of stakeholders, constituents, and families while serving on Executive, Leadership, and Management Teams in local government, a trailblazing and award-winning nonprofit organization serving children and adults with developmental disabilities and special needs, and a historic memorial park serving people from all walks of life including actors, politicians, athletes, soldiers, musicians, artists and entrepreneurs.

Her transition to a life of service as an Author to impart insight, wisdom, and nuggets of truth to trauma survivors and kindred spirits, marks the initiation into the fulfillment of a life mission and purpose embedded in her DNA.

In addition to authoring books, her monthly blog, *Lifelines for Fearless Living*, offers a safe space to explore real life issues with real talk through the heart, mind, and soul of a resourceful and resilient trauma survivor.

As a pusher and peddler of optimism and hope, Lady D is passionate about helping others become who they were born to be in all facets of life.

To learn more about the *mission, core beliefs*, and *compelling message* of Flyte Time Publications you can visit the author's website at www.flytetimepublications.com.

A portion of proceeds from all book sales in the *Life Change Series* will be donated to organizations serving women and girls impacted by trauma and lived experience in foster care.

Your Opinion Matters

If you enjoyed this book or found it useful, please consider posting a review on Amazon.com or other online retailer where you made your purchase. Your support and feedback make a difference in spreading the word about my mission to empower and support trauma survivors.

Upcoming Release Information

To receive updates about the release of **Volume 2,** you can visit my website at **www.flytetimepublications.com** and enter your contact information in the space provided on the webpage, *Connect with Lady D.*

Get Notified!

Blog Subscription

You can subscribe to my monthly blog, *Lifelines for Fearless Living* by entering your contact information on the webpage entitled *Lady D's Blog.*

Subscribe!